Sarapion of Thmuis

Against the Manichaeans
and
Pastoral Letters

Introduced and translated by

Dellas Oliver Herbel

Second Edition

SCD Press
2024

Sarapion of Thmuis:
Against the Manichaeans and Pastoral Letters
(Early Christian Studies, 14, second edition)
Introduced and translated by Dellas Oliver Herbel
© 2011, 2024

SCD Press
PO Box 6110,
Norwest NSW 2153
Australia
scdpress@scd.edu.au

All rights reserved. No part of this book may be reproduced or transmitted in any form or by any means, electronic or mechanical, including photocopying, recording or by any information and storage system without permission in writing from the publishers.

ISBN-13: 978-1-925730-49-4 (paperback)
ISBN-13: 978-1-925730-50-0 (ebook)

Layout and design by: Lankshear Design Pty Ltd
Printed and bound by: Ingram Spark

Sarapion of Thmuis

Against the Manichaeans and *Pastoral Letters*

Introduced and translated by

Dellas Oliver Herbel

Second Edition

SCD Press
2024

Early Christian Studies 14

SCD Press Editorial Board

Professor Stephen Smith

Professor Peter G. Bolt

Professor Constantine R. Campbell

Dr Katherine E. Hurrell

Dr Marguerite Kappelhoff

Early Christian Studies

1. Jan Harm Barkhuizen, *Proclus Bishop of Constantinople. Homilies on the Life of Christ* (2001).
2. Robert C. Hill, *Theodoret of Cyrus. Commentary on the Song of Songs* (2001).
3. Johan Ferreira, *The Hymn of the Pearl* (2002).
4. Alistair Stewart-Sykes, *The Life of Polycarp. An anonymous vita from third-century Smyrna* (2002).
5. Daniel Van Slyke, *Quodvultdeus of Carthage. The Apocalyptic Theology of a Roman African in Exile* (2003).
6. Bronwen Neil & Pauline Allen, *The Life of Maximus the Confessor. Recension 3* (2003).
7. George Kalantzis, *Theodore of Mopsuestia. Commentary on the Gospel of John* (2004).
8. Rudolf Brändle, *John Chrysostom. Bishop – Reformer – Martyr* (2004).
9. J. Mark Armitage, *A Twofold Solidarity. Leo the Great's Theology of Redemption* (2005).
10. Alistair Stewart-Sykes, *The Apostolic Church Order. The Greek Text with Introduction, Translation and Annotation* (2006, 2021).
11. Geoffrey D. Dunn, *Cyprian and the Bishops of Rome: Questions of Papal Primacy in the Early Church* (2007, 2018).
12. Pauline Allen, Majella Franzmann, & Rick Strelan (eds.), *"I Sowed Fruits into Hearts" (Odes Sol. 17:13). Festschrift for Professor Michael Lattke* (2007).
13. David Luckensmeyer & Pauline Allen (eds.), *Studies of Religion and Politics in the Early Christian Centuries* (2010).
14. Dellas Oliver Herbel, *Sarapion of Thmuis: Against the Manichaeans and Pastoral Letters* (2011, 2024).
15. Raymond Laird, *Mindset, Moral Choice and Sin in the Anthropology of John Chrysostom* (2012, 2017).

16. Alexander L. Abecina, *Time and Sacramentality in Gregory of Nyssa's Contra Eunomium* (2013).
17. Johan Ferreira, *Early Chinese Christianity: The Tang Christian Monument and Other Documents* (2014).
18. Wendy Mayer & Ian J. Elmer (eds.), *Men and Women in the Early Christian Centuries* (2014).
19. Silouan Fotineas, *The Letters of Bishop Basil of Caesarea: Instruments of Communion* (2018).
20. Andrey Romanov, *One God as One God and One Lord. The Lordship of Jesus Christ as a Hermeneutical Key to Paul's Christology in 1 Corinthians (with a special focus on 1 Cor 8:6)* (2021).
21. Hyueng Guen Choi, *Charity and the Letters of Barsanuphius and John of Gaza* (2020).
22. Alistair C. Stewart, *The Canons of Hippolytus. An English version, with introduction and annotation and an accompanying Arabic Text* (2021).
23. Peter G. Bolt and Sehyun Kim (eds.), *God's Grace Inscribed on the Human Heart. Essays in Honour of James R. Harrison* (2022).

Preface to the Second Edition

The preface to the first edition of this book noted that many scholars of Christianity, as well as many Christians themselves, knew little, if anything about Sarapion, a bishop and friend of the great St. Athanasius and disciple of St. Anthony the Great. Little has occurred in the intervening years to change that, although my book has helped, as has a subsequent book chapter on Sarapion's hermeneutics. Also, if one performs an internet search, one will encounter some very brief overviews of Sarapion, such as his short Wikipedia entry. Primarily, when referenced, he is seen as a witness to Christianity's early response to Manichaeism or as a witness to an early liturgical tradition. In other words, he is still treated more as an entry point into other topics and figures than as a figure with a *gravitas* all his own. Therefore, this second edition has only needed to receive a minor revision.

Many of Sarapion's writings are no longer extant and none had been translated into English prior to the first edition of this book, except for a partially preserved letter to the disciples of Anthony, written upon Anthony's death. Klaus Fitschen, to whom I am indebted, had possibly done more than anyone else to remedy Sarapion's relative obscurity but further work remained, some of which is addressed here. The two most prominent areas delved into within the introduction to my translations are: Sarapion's hermeneutics and his appropriation of Stoicism (common as that was within early Christianity). While addressing both, I have also highlighted related areas of study, such as the degree to which Sarapion was influenced by the Egyptian religious milieu.

When researching and translating the *Letter to the Monks*, I found myself unconvinced by Fitschen's argument against Sarapion's authorship. I have offered the reader what I believe to be serious counter arguments in favour of Sarapion's authorship. In so doing, I have not only responded to Fitschen's specific objections but also noted similarities to Sarapion's undisputed writings. That said, I have not endeavored to write the final tome of all things Sarapion.

This book originated at St. Vladimir's Orthodox Theological Seminary when I translated the *Letter to Bishop Eudoxius* in order to learn something more about Sarapion. After I began doctoral studies at Saint Louis University, Fr. Frederick G. McLeod took time out of his busy schedule to offer guidance and assistance as I continued my translations. Sadly, he has recently passed away but his dedication to early Christian scholarship will continue to be felt for years to come and I remain thankful for his support.

It is my hope that this work will prove to be a useful introduction to Sarapion and provide people with what is really important, his own words. Many of those words still echo within my own mind and when I look back upon the translation portion of this work, some enjoyable memories come to mind. I am especially fond of the hours I spent holding my son, Micah, an infant at the time, in one hand, while I read and wrote out a translation with the other. In the subsequent years, I have been blessed with two other children, my daughters Macrina and Anastasia, and I am very much indebted to the sacrifices of my entire family, including my wife Lorie. This indebtedness has only increased since I first wrote this, as my academic pursuits have taken a back seat to military chaplaincy. As with that first edition, any remaining mistakes are entirely my own and of no reflection upon family, friends, and colleagues who have helped and supported me.

There are many I could thank for all sorts of things, big and small, but as I did in the preface to the first edition, so I will do here. I shall end by thanking one who is, I believe, above us all. My faith teaches me that I ultimately owe thanksgiving to my Lord and God and Saviour, who works through all the people in my life. On that, I will close with some of Sarapion's own words: "Therefore, thanksgiving is due to the one who has created our bodies, the one who has providentially cared for those who have, themselves, acted heedlessly."

Table of Contents

Preface to the Second Edition ix

Abbreviations 2

Introduction 3

   Sarapion's Historical Context 5

   Against the Manichaeans 17

   Hermeneutics in *Against the Manichaeans* 19

      A Treatise with a Stoic Flare 24

      The Christological Dimension 32

      Concluding Remarks on the Treatise: Free Will, Hermeneutics, and Augustine 34

   The *Letter to Bishop Eudoxius* 42

   The *Letter to the Monks* and the *Adiaphora* of the World 44

      Stoic Terminology 52

      The Monks as Spiritual Descendants of Pharaoh 55

      "Suffering" in the *Letter to the Monks* 59

      The Hermeneutics of the *Letter to the Monks* 59

      Sarapion of Thmuis as the Author of the *Letter to the Monks* 65

Texts in Translation 73

   Letter to Bishop Eudoxius 75

   Letter to the Monks 77

   Against the Manichaeans 89

Select Bibliography 143

Indices 151

Abbreviations

CSEL	Corpus Scriptorum Ecclesiasticorum Latinorum
GCS	Die griechischen christlichen Schriftsteller der ersten Jahrhunderte
LCL	Loeb Classical Library
PG	Patrologia Graeca
SC	Sources Chrétiennes

Introduction

Sarapion's Historical Context

From approximately 329 to 370, Sarapion,[1] disciple of St. Anthony of the desert and ally of St. Athanasius of Alexandria, flourished as the bishop of Thmuis, a city to the east-north-east of Alexandria. Thmuis had assumed, in AD 2, the function of a regional administrative centre and by Sarapion's time was a great city in the Egyptian Nile delta region.[2] Sarapion himself was destined to become a canonised saint of the church.[3]

The first known bishop from Thmuis is Ammonius, who lived there in Origen's time.[4] Phileas, who suffered martyrdom early in Sarapion's lifetime, is the most well know bishop of Thmuis prior to Sarapion. Herbert Musurillo suggests a date for Phileas' death between 304 and the winter of 306/307, while Albert Pietersma claims that Phileas' martyrdom occurred "more specifically between Phileas' involvement with Melitius of Lycopolis in early 306 and the end of Culcianus' term of office".[5] The extant remnants of Phileas' *Letter to the Thmuitians* and the *Letter to Melitius* testify both to Thmuis' municipal status as well as to the establishment of the church and a canonical norm of church order for Egypt (even if Melitius did not feel

---

1. Manuscripts and texts sometimes spell the name Serapion. However, because it is the dominant form of the name and that found on the documents translated here, Sarapion will be used throughout this text except for when quoting from sources preferring Serapion.
2. K. Fitschen, *Serapion von Thmuis: Echte und Unechte Schriften sowie die Zeugnisse des Athanasius und Anderer* (Berlin and New York 1992) 117.
3. Sarapion's commemoration is March 21st. See Хрицтианстро: Энциклопедический Словарь, S.S. Averintsev, A.H. Meshkov, and U.N. Popov (eds.) volume 3 (Moscow 1995) 676.
4. For an interesting discussion concerning whether Ammonios of Thmuis may, in fact, be Ammonios Sakkas, see J.E. Bruns, "Ammonius Sakkas and Ammonius of Thmuis," *Studies in Religion* 4:4 (1974/5) 387–391.
5. H. Musurillo, *The Acts of the Christian Martyrs* (Oxford 1972) xivii. A. Pietersma (ed. and trans.) *The Acts of Phileas, Bishop of Thmuis (Including Fragments of the Greek Psalter)* (Geneva 1984) 14.

obligated to such order).[6] By the year 325, the Melitian schism even divided Christians in Thmuis, with "Ephraim of Thmuis" appearing on a Melitian bishop-list at the same time a Tiberius represented the city at Nicea.[7] Sarapion became Tiberius' direct or indirect successor, becoming the bishop of Thmuis sometime after 325. We know that Sarapion held the bishopric by 339, when he becomes a recipient of a festal letter from Athanasius.[8] Athanasius continued to trust Sarapion's skills as a church leader, which can be ascertained from the fact that on May 19, 353, Sarapion departed Alexandria with a delegation bound for Milan, in order to meet with Constantius II and plead the case of Athanasian orthodoxy.[9] How long Sarapion served as the bishop in Thmuis, we do not know. He had a letter exchange with the future heresiarch Apollinarius in the 370s, which is the last we hear of him, but the list of attendees at the later Council of Constantinople in 381 is incomplete.[10]

Sarapion entered his episcopacy from a monastic background. The *Life of Anthony* testifies that when Anthony the Great died, he bequeathed one of his cloaks to Athanasius and the other to Sarapion.[11] However, the situation remains unclear with respect to which form of

---

6   For a good overview of Phileas, see T. Baumeister, "Der ägyptische Bischof und Märtyrer Phileas," in M. von Stritzky (ed.), *Garten des Lebens Festschrift für Winfrid Cramer* (Altenberge, Germany 1999) 33–41. The *Letter to the Thmuitians* may be found in Musurillo, *The Acts of the Christian Martyrs*, 320–327. The *Acts of Phileas* may also be found in Musurillo, 328–353, although Pietersma provides the most recent and detailed investigation of the text and the manuscripts themselves. F.H. Kettler supplies us with a critical edition of the *Letter to Meletius* in "Der melitianische Streit in Ägypten," *Zeitschrift für die neutestamentliche Wissenschaft und die Kunde der Urchristentums* 35 (1936) 155–193. The critical text may be found at 159–163.
7   Fitschen, *Serapion*, 118.
8   PG 26, 1412–13 contains a Latin translation of the letter, which remains extant only in Syriac.
9   Sozomen, *Ecclesiastical History*, J. Bidez and G.C. Hansen (eds), GCS 50 (Berlin 1960) 4.9.6. See also Sozomen, *Ecclesiastical History*, A. Festugière (trans.), introduction by B. Gillet and G. Sabbah, Greek text edited by J. Bidez, SC 306, 418 (Paris 1983). An English translation is available in Sozomen, *Ecclesiastical History*, in E. Walford (trans.), *The Ecclesiastical History of Sozomen, Comprising a History of the Church from A.D. 324 to A.D. 440. Translated from the Greek: with a Memoir of the Author. Also the Ecclesiastical History of Philostorgius, as Epitomised by Photius* (London 1855).
10   With regard to the letter exchange, we have only brief fragments, which remain in Leontius of Byzantium. Little can be ascertained from them. For a short discussion of them, see Fitschen, *Serapion*, 75–78. Fitschen also notes that the list of the attendees to the council in 381 remains incomplete (149).
11   Athanasius. *Life of Anthony*, in G.J.M. Bartelink (trans. and ed.), *Athanase d'Alexandrie: Vie d'Antoine*, SC 400 (Paris 1994) 91. For an English translation, see R.C. Gregg (trans.), *Athanasius: The Life of Anthony and the Letter to Marcellinus* (New York 1980).

monasticism confronted Sarapion. Toward the end of the fourth century, John Cassian encountered Egyptian monasticism in the East Delta region, which existed in a combination of the anchoretic and coenobitic ways of life and likely went back to Sarapion's time.[12] Indeed, within the vicinity of Thmuis there was a *coenobium* where Cassian met an Abba John.[13]

As a bishop, Sarapion dedicated himself to the well-being of the church. In addition to leading a delegation to Milan in order to meet with Emperor Constantius II, Sarapion invested himself in the liturgical affairs of the church in Thmuis, combated (with the assistance of Athanasius) an early group of Pneumatomachi known as Tropici, wrote an apology against the Manichaeans (relative new-comers to the Egyptian religious scene) and wrote various letters, of which only two are preserved intact, the two translated here (the *Letter to Bishop Eudoxius* and the *Letter to the Monks*[14]). Another, the *Letter on the Death of Anthony*, is partially available in Syriac and Armenian.[15] Fitschen discusses other shorter fragments of Sarapion's letters as well as a few fragments from a commentary on Genesis, which Devreesse also notes.[16] There also remains the possibility that Sarapion authored part or all of the *Life of Anthony* or at least acted as one of the redactors

---

12   Fitschen, *Serapion*, 118.
13   John Cassian, *Collationes XIII*, Michael Petschenig (ed.), Text of the collationes reproduced from 1886 ed., CSEL 13 (Vienna 2004) 14.4. For an English translation, see John Cassian, *Conferences*, C. Luibheid (trans.) (New York 1985).
14   Zirnheld provided a French translation of this letter and a brief introduction in Outtier, B. with A. Louf, M. Van Parys, and Cl.-A. Zirnheld, *Lettres des pères du désert: Ammonas, Macaire, Arsène, Sérapion de Thmuis*. Spiritualité Orientale 42 (Bégrolles en Mauges, Maine & Loire 1985) 116-147.
15   For a French translation of both the Syriac and Armenian versions (inasmuch as they are extant), see Outtier, *Lettres des pères du désert*, 151-157 and also R. Draguet, "Une letter de Sérapion de Thmuis aux disciples d'Antoine (A.D. 356) en version syriaque et arménienne." *Le Muséon* 64 (1951) 1-25. An English translation by Rowan Greer may be found in T. Vivian, and A.N. Athanassakis with R.A. Greer, *The Life of Anthony: The Coptic Life and the Greek Life* (Kalamazoo 2003) 40-47. Oddly, the introduction is but a paragraph long on page 39 and does not even cite Fitschen's work.
16   Fitschen, *Serapion*, 67-78. See also R. Devreesse, *Les anciens commentateurs grecs de l'Octateque et des Rois (fragments tirés des chaines)* (Vatican City 1959) 104. Fragments from the commentary exist in quotations by Severian of Gabala.

of this *Life*.¹⁷

Sarapion may be best known for investing himself in the liturgical affairs of Thmuis through the collection of prayers bequeathed to us under his name. In 1894, Dmitrievskii published a collection of prayers attributed to St. Sarapion of Thmuis, a collection later published by Wobbermin, Brightman, Funk, and, most recently, by Maxwell

---

17   For an important discussion of the authorship of the Life, see B. McNary-Zak, Letters and Asceticism in Fourth-Century Egypt, (Lanham, MD 2000) 88–97, where she suggests it "is a product of the efforts of several people, and that these people were likely Ammonas, Serapion of Thmuis, and to a lesser extent, Athanasius" (95). She provides some important reasons for Sarapion's role in creating this work. First: "there are several words in the *Life of Anthony* that are absent from the vocabulary of Athanasius but are present in the writings of his contemporary, Serapion of Thmuis" (91). In endnote 67, she mentions: "'galania' (stillness), 'exomoioun' (make like), 'hasuxos' (quiet), 'theosebein' (worship god), 'kathareuein' (make clean), and 'kataskeua' (practice)". She also claims the earliest known reference to the Life of Anthony is Sarapion's *Letter to the Monks*. McNary-Zak highlights thematic parallels between these two works, noting the description of "ascetic behavior defined by prayer, ascesis, and combat with demons" (92). Finally: "unlike Athanasius, Serapion of Thmuis would have had a motive for creating this image of Anthony and his ascetic practice. Serapion had a personal interest in maintaining the tradition of Anthony, as evidenced in his *Letter on the Death of Anthony*" (92–93).

However, her arguments in favor of Ammonas do not provide the reader with a compelling case and, in fact, Sarapion's authorship would account for the same concerns! She notes that one function of the *Life of Anthony* would have been to demonstrate "an ideal model for the followers to emulate", which she links to Ammonas' "effort to preserve lineage and to preserve the memory of Anthony" (95). She also says there is solidarity in the two men's teaching and the depiction of the growth and development of ascetic practice is a theme in both Ammonas' letters and the *Life of Anthony*.

McNary-Zak notes that Sarapion must be understood to function within an Antonian-monastic context as well, which includes a master-disciple approach to authority. In light of this and his *Letter on the Death of Anthony*, one need not conjecture the necessity of Ammonas in order to address the issue of Anthony as an "ideal model" in the *Life of Anthony*. After all, McNary-Zak admits that Sarapion would have had a motivation for this as well. She does claim that the depiction of the growth and development of ascetic practice is an argument in Ammonas' favor, but in the section discussing the letters of Anthony and Ammonas (20–39), she presents a significant amount of discontinuity, making it difficult to know exactly what aspect(s) of their presentations of ascetic growth and development prove so consistent and in Ammonas' favor. Even if the consistency were to prove tremendous, this would not necessitate bringing Ammonas into the picture since presumably any devoted follower of Anthony and/or his tradition would have adopted (and at least been aware of) the type of asceticism the Antonian tradition taught. Sarapion should have been as aware of this as any follower of Anthony. Therefore, her insights into Sarapion's role as an author (or at least an important redactor), warrant further exploration.

Johnson.[18] Johnson, in his seminal study of these prayers, argues that of the thirty prayers contained in this manuscript, a group of prayers (2–11, 13, 19, 21, and 24–30) "represents an earlier level of liturgical development in which, for example, a postbaptismal anointing … was not yet known in Egypt, and which also appears to reflect a more primitive understanding of the rite of ordination".[19] In general, Johnson argues that the prayers present us with historical, liturgical development. With regard to the anaphora itself, Johnson says:

> Sarapion's text is an important and potentially reliable witness to the early liturgical tradition. It may provide the structural remains not only of an ancient pattern of eucharistic celebration but also of one way in which the institution narrative itself came to be attached to the anaphora…. Sarapion thus represents preservation.[20]

The unique element of Sarapion's anaphora is also the distinctive aspect of the entire Euchologion—the epiclesis, an epiclesis not of the Holy Spirit, but of the Word. Johnson claims "there is no question but that Sarapion's epiclesis of the λόγος in both the anaphora and the prayer for the sanctification of the baptismal waters (prayer 7) is the great *crux interpretum* for the liturgical, theological, and historical contexts of the document as a whole".[21] Johnson argues that there is

---

18   See, respectively: A. Dmitrievskii, "Евхологион IV века Сарапиона, епископа Тмуитскаго," Труды, Киевской духовной академии 2 (1894) 242-274. G. Wobbermin, *Altchristliche liturgische Stücke aus der Kirche Aegyptens nebst einem dogmatischen Brief des Bischofs Serapion von Thmuis* (Leipzig and Berlin, 1898). F.E. Brightman, "The sacramentary of Serapion," *Journal of Theological Studies* 1 (1900) 88-113, 247-277. F.X. Funk, *Didascalia et Constitutiones Apostolorum*, vol. 2 (Paderborn 1905) 158-203. M.E. Johnson, *The Prayers of Sarapion of Thmuis: A Literary, Liturgical, and Theological Analysis* (Rome 1995).
19   Johnson, *Prayers*, 199.
20   Ibid., 233.
21   Ibid., 234.

good reason to believe that the epiclesis is ancient[22] and Johnson summarises his finding by stating that "what Sarapion expresses in a liturgical form is consistent with an archaic christological understanding, a theology of the λόγος as old as Justin Martyr and still operative to some extent in Athanasius....the most logical conclusion is that the epiclesis of the λόγος also represents the preservation, or at least the remnant, of an earlier euchological form".[23]

Sarapion is also known from the letters that Athanasius wrote to him concerning the Holy Spirit. Sometime during 358 or 359, Sarapion of Thmuis wrote to Athanasius (in exile at the time) informing him of a group of Christians in Thmuis known as the Tropici (Christians who, in many respects, anticipate the later Pneumatomachi of the late fourth century).[24] Michael A.G. Haykin, although acknowledging the possible inaccuracy to the arguments against which Athanasius contends in his *Letters to Sarapion concerning the Divinity of the Holy Spirit*, claims that some general points can be ascertained. The most significant would be that the Tropici declared that the Holy Spirit is a creature of angelic nature.[25] Since Athanasius does not call them heretics immediately in the first letter and Sarapion writes asking advice, "it can be assumed that, at this point, there was a dialogue between the Nicene community and the Pneumatomachi of Thmuis".[26] Haykin also notes that this is the first group to whom the name Pneumatomachi may be given.[27] C.R.B. Shapland, in the introduction to his translation of the letters, notes that the Tropici have a clearly

---

22 As evidence, he cites a sermon excerpt from Athanasius where Athanasius speaks of the Word descending upon the bread and wine, notes that the first Egyptian reference to the descent of the Holy Spirit is during the Alexandrian pontificate of St. Peter II (373–80), and highlights the work of Ezra Gebremedhin, who claims that even for St. Cyril of Alexandria the λόγος is the principle agent in the act of consecration. He also presents the reader with supporting patristic references from Ss. Justin Martyr, Irenaeus, and Clement of Alexandria, as well as Origen. In each of these cases, the patristic author parallels the incarnation of Christ with the transformation of the Eucharistic elements. Finally, he notes the work of Sebastian Brock on the ancient Antiochene baptismal ordines, where the original formula seems to have asked Christ to "come" upon the water.
23 Ibid., 253.
24 M.A.G. Haykin, *The Spirit of God: The Exegesis of 1 and 2 Corinthians in the Pneumatomachian Controversy of the Fourth Century* (Leiden and New York 1994) 20–21.
25 Ibid., 21.
26 Ibid., 22.
27 Ibid., 20.

defined line of argumentation, with the divinity of the Father and Son unquestioned and the created status (by way of the Son) of the Holy Spirit likewise an uncompromising feature.[28] Furthermore, Shapland argues that Athanasius writes "as though, through Serapion, he were addressing a body of teachers and pastors toward whom he had special responsibilities, and who naturally looked to him for guidance and instruction".[29] In other words, the issue appears to be a diocesan one (for Thmuis), and certainly not expanding beyond the purview of the patriarchate of Alexandria. The fact that the Tropici are not mentioned again in the history of the church as part of the larger Pneumatomachian movement supports Shapland's contention.

In light of the liturgical tradition of Thmuis, both the Tropici's clear demarcation between the Son and the Holy Spirit and the movement's limitation to the diocese of Thmuis raises the possibility that the traditional theology of Thmuis upheld a clear connection of divinity between God the Father and his Son but presented ambiguity concerning God's relationship to his Spirit (allowing for two parties—one that upheld the full divinity of the Spirit and one that believed he was the highest of the angels). To be sure, the evidence presents only a circumstantial case, but a strong circumstantial case, that prior to Sarapion, Thmuitians held to a liturgical and theological tradition that emphasised the work of the λόγος and remained ambiguous concerning the place of the Holy Spirit. Given that the late fourth century was a time of much debating concerning the role of the Spirit, such an observation may seem germane and somewhat trite. However, it is still worth noting that Christianity in Thmuis was traditionally divided over the status of the Spirit and until the episcopal oversight of Sarapion, remained a "conservative" locale, possibly even retaining its Logocentric liturgical practices during and after Sarapion's episcopacy.

The letter exchange with Athanasius raises the question of whether

28 C.R.B. Shapland, *The Letters of Saint Athanasius Concerning the Holy Spirit* (London 1951), 28-29. See also K. Anatolios, *Athanasius* (London 2004) 212, where Anatolios notes that the Tropici considered the Holy Spirit to be unlike the Father and 30, where Anatolios notes that Athanasius specifically claims in his letters to Sarapion that the Holy Spirit is *homoousios* with the Father. Anatolios provides a translation of the second half of the first letter on pages 214-233. Despite the importance of these letters, no one has yet published a critical text (Anatolios, *Athanasius*, 214).
29 Ibid., 27.

Sarapion had been a confessor for the faith. According to Jerome, Sarapion was, in fact, a confessor during the struggles with Arianism, suggesting he fled from Thmuis.[30] However, Fitschen notes that Athanasius does not include Sarapion among those who had to flee their sees and that Sarapion clearly corresponded with Athanasius regarding the Tropici in Thmuis sometime during the years 358–60.[31] Fitschen suggests, therefore, that "confessor" had a rather broad connotation for Jerome, which would have made the term applicable as a title of honour, exalting those, such as Sarapion, who significantly participated in the fight on behalf of the true faith.[32] If this is the case, then it would seem highly likely that in the mid to late fourth century Thmuis was a see with three bishop-claimants—one a Melitian, one an Arian, and one orthodox.

As if dealing with a Melitian schism, Arianism, and an early group of Pneumatomachi were not enough, Sarapion also faced Manichaeans. Manichaean missionaries reached Alexandria in 270.[33] Manichaeism understood history to consist of three epochs (the beginning, middle, and end) in which the two kingdoms (one of light and one of darkness) battle each other.[34] The kingdom of light includes twelve aeons, which are hypostases of the father of light, while the kingdom of dark-

---

30 See Jerome, *On Illustrious Men*, T.P. Halton (trans.), (Washington, DC 1999) 99. See also I. Hilberg (ed.), *Sancti Eusebii Hieronymi Epistulae* (Vienna 1996) 70.4.4.
31 Fitschen, *Serapion*, 148.
32 Ibid.
33 Ibid., 7.
34 S.N.C. Lieu, *Manichaeism in the Later Roman Empire and Medieval China* (Tübingen 1992) 10-11. M. Tardieu also provides a summary of Manichaeism in *Le Manichéisme* (Paris 1981), though he offers no significant discussion of Manichaean soteriology. Widengren had discussed soteriology previously. See G. Widengren, *Mani and Manichaeism* (London 1965). For a brief overview of Manichaean sources, see J.D. BeDuhn, *The Manichaean Body* (Baltimore and London: 2000) 2-4 and I. Gardner and S.N.C. Lieu, *Manichaean Texts from the Roman Empire* (Cambridge 2004) 35-45. With respect to Manichaean dualism, as evidenced by the belief in the two kingdoms (that of the light and that of the dark), it should be noted that scholars have debated whether and to what extent Manichaeism may be monotheistic rather than completely dualistic. For a summary of much of the debate and a via media argument, which claims that Manichaeism simultaneously upheld "an ontological dualism and a theological monotheism," see C.G. Scibona, "How monotheistic is Mani's dualism? Once more on monotheism and dualism in Manichaean gnosis," *Numen: International Review for the History of Religions* 48:4 (2001) 444-467.

ness includes five evil archons.[35] Darkness is a state of random motion and attacked the light, while the father of light replied with consubstantial manifestations of himself.[36] Darkness trapped some of the elements of light, but in so doing, fell into a trap of the father of light who was willing to sacrifice some of his troops in order to win the larger war itself.[37] The eventual end of this struggle will be "the ultimate 'apokatastasis'" of the unredeemed light elements.[38]

Manichaeans held some doctrinal positions that have a more direct relevance to Sarapion's own treatise. They believed "the human body is evil because it was created out of the five great powers of Darkness. But the soul, though being Light itself, can nevertheless sin through forgetting its divine origin".[39] One of the implications of this approach is that "sin, from the Manichaean point of view, is not an act of one's own volition but a temporary loss of consciousness by the soul".[40] The Manichaean dependence upon previous Marcionite arguments is like-

---

35 Lieu, *Manichaeism*, 11–12. However, it should be noted that Manichaeans could downplay the importance of their mythology when it suited their evangelistic purposes. See N.A. Pedersen, *Demonstrative Proof in Defence of God: A Study of Titus of Bostra's Contra Manichaeos, the Work's Sources, Aims and Relation to its Contemporary Theology* (Leiden and Boston 2004) 161, where Pedersen observes that in the case of the Manichaeans to whom Alexander of Lycopolis responds, "the names of the Manichaean gods/hypostasisings of the deity are for the most part replaced by philosophical concepts". BeDuhn suggests, "the term *syncretism* scarcely does justice to a movement so self-consciously absorbent, so openly adaptive as we know the Manichaeans to have been. … To try to hold together a unified Manichaean tradition in the face of such striking mutability in the sources is a tall order" (6). BeDuhn's observations prove all too true when viewing the entire historical and geographical distribution of Manichaeism (which survived in China until at least the fifteenth century), though even his project seeks to ascertain the "core" of Manichaeism (7).
36 Lieu, *Manichaeism*, 13–14.
37 Ibid., 14–15.
38 Ibid., 17. Lieu also describes the sexual activities of the demons and the role of Adam and Eve and Jesus the Luminous' role of waking Adam from his sleep within this cosmic struggle (18–22).
39 Ibid., 24. It should be noted that although it is largely true, from an ontological standpoint, that they believed the body to be evil, Manichaeans did believe the body could be used for good purposes, at least as a means to further serve in the redemption of light. Pedersen notes the importance of ethical commandments and responsibility despite the fact that one could logically deduce determinism from the Manichaeans' own ontological premises (173–174). Also, BeDuhn argues that although all surviving Manichaean accounts claim that humanity was created as instruments of evil (88), by mastering the body, Manichaeans could live out the victory of light over darkness (97).
40 Ibid., 25.

wise important.⁴¹ Additional Manichaean teachings relevant to Sarapion's treatise are the Manichaean beliefs in reincarnation and an eschatological conflagration.⁴²

Prior to Sarapion's writing of *Against the Manichaeans*, Egypt produced at least two written responses to the Manichaeans. Bishop Theonas of Alexandria possibly produced the first. The response is an epistle rather than a treatise and likely dates from the late third century, which would place it within the timeframe of Theonas' jurisdiction.⁴³ Theonas' name does not appear on the manuscript as we have it, but both the time of the edict of Diocletian against the Manichaeans and the orthography would suggest a late third-century writing and the lack of any personal character suggest its intended use as an official document.⁴⁴ The argumentation concerns morality more than cosmology or the philosophical elements of Manichaeism. Theonas notes that the Manichaeans reject marriage, claiming they revere the menstrual blood of some of their elect.⁴⁵ He also speaks of Manichaeans as madmen, playing upon a possible pun one may note, in Greek, between Mani, the name of the religion's founder, and μανία or madness.⁴⁶ Two other points worth mentioning are his claim that Manichaeans worship creation and that Manichaeans steal into Christian houses with

---

41 Lieu claims: "Marcion's influence on Mani is both profound and pervasive ... the arguments adduced by the Manichaeans against the Old Testament are often the same as those of the Marcionites ... One disciple of Mani, by the name of Addā (Lat. Adimantus), would even model the format of his anti-Old Testament work on the *Antitheses* of Marcion" (53). See also chapter three, where Lieu discusses this work of Addā. However, Lieu also claims: "the Catholics would argue that the Old Testament had to be retained because the Mosaic laws were fundamental to the moral precepts of a Christian society. Furthermore ... it was needed as proof of his divinity [because of prophecy]" (155). In response, the Manichaean Faustus claims that he could find no prophecies (Lieu, 156). Lieu cites Augustine's *Contra Faustus* XII, 1. Pedersen likewise notes that the Manichaean opponents of Titus of Bostra relied upon Marcionite argumentation (216–224).
42 Ibid., 29–30.
43 C.H. Roberts, (ed.), *Catalogue of the Greek and Latin Papyri in the John Rylands Library, Manchester*, vol. 3, theological and literary texts, nos. 457–551 (Manchester 1938), no. 469, 38–46. For ease of reference, the author will be designated "Theonas," with the caveat that presently it cannot be "proven" that he wrote the epistle.
44 Ibid., 38.
45 Ibid., 42.
46 Ibid. This attack may be found throughout anti-Manichaean literature. Sarapion himself uses it in *Against the Manichaeans* 3.23, where he speaks of "the insanity (μανία) of Mani" and it may be found in many other authors including Titus of Bostra, Eusebius, and Theodoret of Cyrus (see Pedersen, *Titus of Bostra*, 130, 137–138, and 168).

deceitful and lying words.[47]

47 Roberts, *Papyri*, 42. In light of recent discussions about labeling Manichaeism "Christian," it should be noted that throughout this project, whether discussing Manichaeism generally or Theonas' accusation specifically (one that Sarapion will also use), I present Christianity and Manichaeism as two separate religions. Lieu prefers to use the term "Catholics" for Christians in order to avoid having to classify Manichaeans as either "Christian" or "non-Christian." Strousma claims that Manichaeans were Christians. See G.G. Strousma, "The Manichaean challenge to Egyptian Christianity," in B.A. Pearson and J.E. Goehring (eds), *The Roots of Egyptian Christianity* (Philadelphia 1986) 308, where he writes: "one cannot see the conflict between Manichaeism and Christianity as a conflict between two independent religions." Pedersen likewise adopts the term "Catholics" for those Christians who opposed the Gnostics, Arians, et. al., and prefers to see Manichaeans as Christians, seeking to understand "Christian" in a broad sense (6–13). This raises an important question. What is actually gained by simply renaming groups along the same fault lines? Pedersen does provide an answer to this question. He says: "the paramount concern is to avoid a terminology that tears apart groups and ideas which in a historical perspective had not only a common source [they all appeal to Jesus as a central figure, if not the central figure, in some sort of way] but also a continuous, interconnected history in which they remained related: each defined itself in relation to the other and each professed to represent the true version of what its opponent also claimed to be … theological valuation lies on a different level from the historical" (11). There should be no doubting that Manichaeism has what we might term Judeo-Christian Gnostic roots. See J.C. Reeves, *Heralds of that Good Realm: Syro-Mesopotamian Gnosis and Jewish Traditions* (Leiden and New York 1996) and M. Franzmann, *Jesus in the Manichaean Writings* (London 2003). However, I see numerous problems with Pedersen's position. First, why are theological evaluations inherently inadmissible while others are not? Second, how does one successfully keep within this non-theological "norm" of historical study by simply renaming along the same fault lines? To call Christians "Catholics" in distinction from other "Christians," such as Manichaeans and Gnostics, maintains a "theological valuation." Third, the appeal to a "common source" stretches the evidence, for it requires referring to all groups utilizing a Jesus figure as "Christian" without allowing for an analysis of *how* the Jesus figure functions for each group. Jesus' role for the Manichaeans, as portrayed by Franzmann, differs radically from the role Jesus plays for orthodox Christianity. See J. Behr, *The Way to Nicaea* (Crestwood, NY 2003). Finally, there is the importance of Manichaeian indebtedness to thought systems beyond Jewish and Christian Gnosticism. For a recent example, see M. Ataç, "Manichaeism and ancient Mesopotamian 'gnosticism,'" *Journal of Ancient Near Eastern Religions* 5:1 (2005) 1–39. I am fully aware that I am contradicting a current trend in early church scholarship, which prefers to see an overlapping reality rather than communities with self-conscious, distinctive identities. For a defence of the overlapping not of Gnostics and Christians, but of Jews and Christians, see D. Boyarin, *Border Lines: The Partition of Judeo-Christianity* (Philadelphia 2004). However, I am extremely hesitant to discard Christianity and Manichaeism as labels of distinction. I readily admit that overlap occurred among some adherents, much as how a Roman Catholic might attend a Pentecostal Bible study today, for why else would both Theonas and Sarapion accuse Manichaeans of infiltrating Christianity? However, because of the concerns just raised and because Sarapion himself believed he was writing about two different religious communities, I retain "Christian" and "Manichaean" as exclusive labels throughout this work. In the ensuing years since the first edition, interest in the relationship between Christianity and Manichaeanism has only continued. See Johannes van Oort, ed., *Manichaeism and Early Christianity: Selected Papers from the 2019 Pretoria Congress and Consultation* (Leiden and Boston 2021).

The second response to Manichaean evangelisation came from Alexander of Lycopolis. Although Photios, patriarch of Constantinople in the late ninth century, presents Alexander as the bishop of Lycopolis, the scholarly consensus since Brinkman published his critical Greek text claims that Alexander was a Platonist only and not a Platonic Christian.[48] The treatise dates from sometime before 300.[49] Alexander argues against the Manichaean notion of two principles (God and matter), proceeding with a philosophical case against them, noting that the Manichaeans must end up with four principles, as each principle, being productive, must produce another principle.[50] He also notes that two extremes cannot mix[51] and that humanity has the power of discrimination and moral progress.[52] Interestingly, Alexander also asks, near the end of his treatise, why it is that Manichaeans do not accept "the so-called ancient history," if they claim Christ, a possible reference to their rejection of the Scriptures of the Old Testament.[53]

---

48 P.W. van der Horst and J. Mansfeld, *An Alexandrian Platonist Against Dualism: Alexander of Lycopolis' Treatise 'Critique of the Doctrines of Manichaeus'* (Leiden 1974) 3. Van der Horst and Mansfeld note that C. Riggi does argue that Alexander is a Christian, but they find Riggi's arguments unconvincing. See Riggi's work, *Una testimonianza del "kerygma" cristiano in Alessandro di Licopoli, Salesianum* 31 (1969) 561–628.
49 Ibid., 4.
50 Ibid., 58–60.
51 Ibid., 66.
52 Ibid., 43–46, 78–79.
53 Ibid., 92.

Against the Manichaeans

Sarapion's primary writing endeavour consisted of his treatise *Against the Manichaeans*.[54] One cannot precisely date this work. Sarapion does not highlight any events contemporary with his writing of the piece other than a general infiltration of Egypt and Christianity by Manichaeans. Therefore, the manner in which Sarapion discusses Trinitarian theology becomes the most helpful clue. Sarapion uses the term ὁμοούσιος but once, and in that case, it has nothing to do with Trinitarian theology, but simply to help Sarapion make the point that the apostles "had come into being from the one who had made them, not as co-essential (ὁμοούσια) with the one who had made them".[55] Fitschen notes that Sarapion does use the term ὅμοιος to show similarity in nature but not because of any particular Trinitarian position.[56] Because of this, the treatise almost certainly predates the heightened environs of the Arian conflict.[57] Fitschen suggests that because the treatise does not deal with any specific monastic concerns, Sarapion may well have already been a bishop and so the treatise probably dates from sometime after 326.[58] There is no reason to argue with Fitschen on this score. Therefore, Sarapion provides us with the earliest Christian treatise against the Manichaeans.

Sarapion's treatise has some overlap with Theonas' letter and Alexander's treatise, but not extensively. With regard to Theonas' letter, Sarapion speaks to the infiltration of Christianity by the Manichaeans:

> Since, therefore, many wolves (clothed in the fleeces of sheep) have come forward (προῆλθον), let the shepherd's knowledge not be kept secret (μὴ σιωπάτω), but let him shake the sword of the Word, warding off danger for the nurslings and fighting on behalf of the flock striving for the

---

54 For the critical Greek text, see R.P. Casey, "Serapion of Thmuis against the Manichees," *Harvard Theological Studies* 15, published as an extra number of the *Harvard Theological Review* (1931). All citations from *Against the Manichaeans* refer to this text.
55 *Against the Manichaeans*, 27.6.
56 Fitschen, *Serapion*, 11.
57 On this, see also M. West, "Serapion of Thmuis. Between Origen and Athanasius", *Studia Patristica* 42 (2006) 273–276, who also suggests an early date for the treatise.
58 Ibid., 13.

security for the flock, but also revealing the attack of the wild animals. For behold! There are many who have come forward and they wander here and there, having worn the name of Christ (τὸ ὄνομα τοῦ Χριστοῦ περιβεβλημένοι) (in the place of fleeces) and calling themselves something they are not (but being something they refuse to be called). Hiding their own evil behind the dignity of the name and uniting with the name, but striving to destroy completely the name of Christ, they fight against Jesus while calling upon Jesus (κατὰ μὲν τοῦ Ἰησοῦ στρατευόμενοι, Ἰησοῦν δὲ ἐπικεκλημένοι)![59]

Although Sarapion does not specifically mention deceitful and lying words, this passage from Sarapion's treatise comes on the heels of his opening discussion of evil and deceit, and clearly the Manichaeans of whom Sarapion here speaks were masquerading as true Christians, using the names "Jesus" and "Christ" while not adhering to what Sarapion knows to be orthodox Christianity.

Sarapion does not borrow anything from Alexander, at least not anything specific, although they both share some general concerns, such as ridiculing the Manichaean notion of two eternal principles, or causes. Sarapion devotes significant portions of his treatise to the question Alexander raises in passing: why do the Manichaeans not accept the ancient writings of the Scriptures if they claim to be Christians? Sarapion shares Alexander's concern with free will and moral responsibility, but he develops his argument from a Christianised Stoic perspective rather than Alexander's Neo-Platonic approach.

In fact, these two facets (the hermeneutical question and a Christianised Stoicism) become Sarapion's two central themes and give shape to his thought throughout. Sarapion's exegesis grounds his entire exercise, especially when he responds to the Manichaeans' disdain for the Law, the Psalms, and the Prophets. The Stoic influences combine with his exegetical approach to emphasise free will and moral responsibility.

---

59 *Against the Manichaeans*, 3.5–14.

Hermeneutics in *Against the Manichaeans*

One of the most notable features of Sarapion's biblical interpretation is the manner in which he distinguishes what we call the Old and New Testaments.[60] For Sarapion, the Old Testament receives either the designation of Scripture (τὰ γεγραμμένα) or "ancient things" (τὰ παλαιά), whereas the New Testament writings consistently receive the designation of "oracles" (τὰ λογία). The one exception to this occurs in section forty-four, where Sarapion claims the Law banishes "cowardice by saying the oracle (διὰ τοῦ λέγοντος λογίου), 'Do not fear when a man may be enriched. Do not fear the reproach of men and do not be overcome by their contempt.'"[61] In this case, a Psalm verse receives the designation "oracle".

The distinction between Scripture/ancient things and oracles forges the backbone to Sarapion's attack against the Manichaean disdain for the Law, the Psalms, and the Prophets. Sarapion labels the Gospels (and indeed all of the New Testament citations he provides) "oracles" because they utter the message that resides within the Law, Psalms, and Prophets:

> [I]f they say the Law did not reveal and the Prophets did not proclaim, they who utter against what was foreseen will be refuted. Whereby we are not devising their refutation, but the Gospels themselves are publicly speaking against them (αὐτῶν εὐαγγελίων φανερῶς φθεγγομένων) here and there, by crying out somewhere, "so that what was spoken through Isaiah the prophet might be fulfilled"[62] and somewhere else, "I came not to destroy the Law, but to fulfil it".[63]

Here, Sarapion directly links the utterance of the oracles of the Gospels to the message that exists in the Law and the Prophets, citing verses from Matthew to sustain his case.

---

60 In addition to what is said here, also see my "A 'Doctrine of Scripture' from the Eastern Orthodox Tradition: A Reflection on the Desert Father Sarapion of Thmuis" in *What is the Bible? The Patristic Doctrine of Scripture*, edited by Matthew Baker and Mark Mourachian (Minneapolis: Fortress Press, 2016) 21–34.
61 *Against the Manichaeans*, 44.25. Ps 48:17 (49:16).
62 Matt 4:14. See also Matt 12:17.
63 *Against the Manichaeans*, 40.21–26. Matthew 5:17.

This contrasts sharply with his presentation of the Manichaean approach. For "they invoke the Gospel by name, not having preserved the corpus of the Gospel as a corpus, but they have made, according to their own desires, another corpus of Scriptures, even going so far as to take over the name 'Gospel'".[64] This is precisely why the Manichaeans "utter contrary things". Because they do not have the Scriptures and the oracles, they forge their own Scriptures (which include portions of their own liking from the true oracles) and become their own oracles. Christians, on the other hand, have the Scriptures and so they have the oracles and need not proclaim themselves, but may proclaim the true oracles, which in turn utter the true message of the Law and Prophets.

Sarapion even goes so far as to discuss this exegetical reality as a hypothesis:

> And someone will have power over angels and archangels and the other powers, and over heaven and earth, and the other creations when he has investigated [all of this] in order to behold the similarity (ὁμοιότητα) of the Law and the Gospel, thus extending [this activity] to the smallest detail. We, however, refuse so great a dignity, having only furnished what is needful for the hypothesis (ὑποθέσει) and encouraging those eager for knowledge, who have held fast to the hypothesis, to advance toward all the things that are beheld.[65]

Although Sarapion claims that he and his readers are not advancing to the great extent of the dignity available to those who understand the similarity of the Law and the Gospel, he does claim that such similarity is the Christian hypothesis that one brings to the Bible. In this section, Sarapion is discussing the similarity between the Law and Gospel with respect to ethical requirements and the bestowing of mercy, but in light of the rest of the treatise, he clearly means something more.

For, in addition both to designating the New Testament writings as the "oracles" proclaiming the message of the Scriptures and to claiming

---

64 *Against the Manichaeans* 36.17–21.
65 *Against the Manichaeans* 48.65–49.3. In light of the reference to beholding the similarity of the Law and the Gospel, "all the things that are beheld," almost certainly refers to similarities between the Law and the Gospel that Sarapion does not take the time to investigate.

that the hypothesis for approaching the Bible is the similarity of the Law and Gospel, Sarapion directs the reader to what certainly must be that hypothesis—the risen Christ. According to Sarapion, what ultimately links the Scriptures and the oracles is that the economies of Christ are the message of the Scriptures and the proclamation uttered by the oracles:

> In short, if someone gathering up the prophesies from the Law would wish to bring together the entire Gospel, in this way writing down the things that have been effected through prophetic words, he will reveal himself to be someone fond of learning and studious of words, one who exegetes (not apart from the Spirit) his instructions, his teachings, his baptism, the fulfilment of signs, the judgment that came to pass, the betrayal by Judas, the plan of salvation (οἰκονομίαν) on the erect scaffolding, the gall and vinegar given to him in his thirst, the burial itself, and the tomb, the transaction (οἰκονομίαν) in Hades, the Resurrection itself, and, finally, the Ascension. Then, henceforth, he will also cry, "Lift up the gates you rulers, and be lifted up, everlasting gates, and the king of glory will come in".[66] And then this one will also add what has been written by David: "The Lord said to my Lord, 'Sit at my right hand until I make your enemies your footstool.'"[67]
>
> Therefore, if the Law accurately described the coming of the Son and transmitted this long ago, the law is no longer discredited and is no longer attributed to another. The one who has begotten has announced beforehand. The one who determined through his Word[68] preconceived the circumstances. God has begotten, God says, "You are my Son; today I have begotten you".[69] God dispatched. God spoke through Moses: "The Lord God will raise up a prophet for you from amongst your brethren. You will

---

66   Ps 23:7 (24:7).
67   Ps 109:1 (110:1).
68   Although West notes that "Son" is used more frequently than "Word", the latter term still functions in an important manner for Sarapion, especially when one considers Sarapion's hermeneutics. See West, "Serapion of Thmuis", 275.
69   Ps 2:7.

listen to him even so far as everything he may say to you".[70] God determined and, while determining, he did not keep silent. He indicated his will beforehand, producing faith through the things he indicated beforehand. He says, "for his name is called messenger of great counsel, wonderful counsellor, ruler of peace, Father of the ages to come".[71]

To put it simply: the economies of Christ are the true subject matter of the Law, Psalms, and Prophets.

That the economies of Christ are the subject matter of the Law and Prophets should come as no surprise since the Son/Word of God is the author of them in the first place:

> For if "no one knows the things of God except the Spirit of God",[72] and the one writing the Law knew the things of God and knew as much as God determined and, on account of this, has written from observation and understanding, the one writing, then, was from God and was God and was in God and, on account of this, God has spoken however much he determined.[73]

The author of the Scriptures "was from God and was God and was in God", and so we can be sure of his message. As the Word of God, the Son utters on behalf of the Father, as was the case even in Jesus' earthly ministry. For when relating the example of Jesus' rebuke of Peter after the latter had received the keys to the Kingdom of Heaven for his confession of faith, Sarapion says, "he had just received the keys of heaven since the Father uttered through Jesus 'Peter' instead of 'Simon'"![74]

One should not think that the matter is simply that the Manichaeans do not know that the economies of Christ are the hypothesis linking the Scriptures and the oracles. This is certainly the main thrust behind Sarapion's biblical argument. However, Sarapion's hermeneutic works in a circular manner. If it is important to note that the Law actually writes of the economies of Christ and that the Gospels

---

70 Deut 18:15-16a.
71 *Against the Manichaeans* 40.59-80. Isa 9:6.
72 1 Cor 2:11.
73 *Against the Manichaeans* 40.27-31.
74 Ibid., 23.13-14.

are the oracles on behalf of those economies, then it is likewise important to note that Sarapion's hermeneutic simultaneously goes the other way, that it circles back upon itself. "For the silence of the Law is ignorance concerning what is being proclaimed, but knowledge of the Lawgiver is full knowledge of what is declared beforehand."[75] Sarapion's predominate approach throughout the treatise is to argue the movement from the Law through the Gospels, but one should not underestimate this statement here, that it is knowledge of the Lawgiver (the Word who authored the Scriptures) that opens the Scriptures to their meaning. Sarapion even goes on to say:

> For behold, the eisegetes of truth (τῆς ἀληθείας εἰσηγηταί), having honoured the Law, exegeted the Law, while these people, having slandered the Law, skirmish with the Law and quarrel with those who exegete the Law. The apostles know the exact similarity of the Gospel and the Law and taking up the Law, they see the Gospel and, looking in the Gospel, they do not rescind the Law, but these people, are those who always considered similar things dissimilar, and who profess things friendly towards themselves to be implacable hostile sisters.[76]

The apostles, because they have the correct hypothesis when they read the Bible, see the Gospel in the Law in addition to seeing the Law in the Gospel. Upon the correct hypothesis (that the Scriptures and oracles relate the same economies of Christ) one enters the Christian hermeneutical circle. By rejecting the Scriptures, the Manichaeans cannot do this, and so, they are "false Christians" (ψευδόχριστοι).[77]

---

75 Ibid. 36.35-37.
76 48.46-53. Though not explicitly noted, the "implacable, hostile sisters" are almost certainly the Law and the Gospel.
77 Ibid., 54.2. Sarapion's hermeneutic presents a different argument on behalf of the Old Testament than those Lieu claims the catholic church used (that the Old Testament provided moral precepts fundamental to a Christian society and that the prophecies prove Christ's divinity). Although Sarapion's hermeneutic might appear close to Lieu's second argument, Sarapion does not use the ancient Scriptures to demonstrate the divinity of Christ. Rather, Sarapion claims that the ancient Scriptures proclaim the Gospel. They are written about Christ and his economies, the message that the oracles of the New Testament utter. The ancient writings are necessary for understanding who Christ is as a person, not for understanding a particular aspect of his person (such as his divinity).

A Treatise with a Stoic Flare

In addition to the hermeneutical thrust of the treatise, Sarapion adds a philosophical thrust, a Stoic one. Some of the most obvious examples of this influence may be found from sections 44 through 47, where Sarapion discusses the Law in relation to virtue and vice. Section 44 opens with the four traditional Stoic vices.

> Because the Law destroyed every form of evil and did not overlook one portion, but proceeded against every portion of evil, restraining and destroying it, it is clear from the conditions concerning evil that there are four forms of evil: imprudence (ἀφροσύνης), intemperance (ἀκολασίας), cowardice (δειλίας), and injustice (ἀδικίας).[78]

In section 47, he mentions the four Stoic virtues.

> For there exist four virtues: prudence (φρονήσεως), self-control (σωφροσύνης), courage (ἀνδρείας), and righteousness (δικαιοσύνης). The virtues are entirely within the Law.[79]

Malcom Schofield notes that Strobaeus provides us with the four central virtues and their corresponding vices, which Strobaeus claims to have been elicited from Zeno.[80] They formed the backbone to the Stoic task of living according to nature.[81]

In sections 29 and 30, Sarapion discusses Hades, which he describes as a place of finite duration and a place of correction. Sarapion's opening sentences of section 30 prove interesting on this point:

> Besides, the same abyss is a torture-chamber (βασανιστήριον) and a place of correction (κολαστήριον), yet not everlasting and uncreated (οὐκ αἰώνιον δὲ οὔτε ἀγένητον), but having been created at some later time, having been made sometime later as a cure (φαρμάκου) and a remedy (βοηθήματος) for those who have sinned. For holy are the

---

78 Ibid., 44.3-4.
79 Ibid., 47.11.
80 Malcom Schofield, "Stoic ethics," in B. Inwood (ed.), *The Cambridge Companion to the Stoics* (Cambridge 2003) 239.
81 Ibid., 239-246, where Schofield discusses these virtues and vices within the context of "following nature."

scourges that are a cure for those who have sinned. Holy are the blows that are a remedy befalling those who have fallen. For the blows occur not in order that they might become evil, but rather, the scourgings occur in order that they might not become evil. For the evil ones who are distressed by the blows reduce their evil through the scourging. Because of this, we do not complain of the abyss but rather know that it has been created to be a torture-chamber and a place of correction, that is, a means of teaching self-control (σωφρονισμός) to those who have sinned.[82]

According to Sarapion, Hades serves the function of correction and teaching self-control, one of the central Stoic virtues. Sarapion even applies such correction to the demons.[83]

For Sarapion, Hades does not exist as an eternal reality, inflicting the never-ending punishment of a relentless God. Rather, the context is one of God shaping and redeeming all of creation:

> For self-control (σωφροσύνη), being an act, testifies to a self-controlled (σώφρονος) body and the oracles (λόγια), shouting and saying, "present your bodies as a living sacrifice, acceptable to God,"[84] make sufficient proof. For God neither accepts what is not his own nor demands what has been created by another, so that he himself might not become violent (βίαιος), demanding violence (βίαν) against others, and so that he might not covet something belonging to another, as if he could not create it himself. For if it is honourable, and he wishes bodies to be self-controlled (σωφρονεῖν), how could he not make what he wished?[85]

God is not a God of everlasting violence. The God who creates pursues his creation, even to the depths of Hades, never ceasing to change and correct each creature. If one wishes to speak of a relentless God, then it

---

82 *Against the Manichaeans* 30.1–9.
83 Ibid., 29–30. Sarapion actually raises the issue of Hades in light of his discussion of Jesus' encounter with demons. Sections 29 and 30 both address the need for the demons to be corrected.
84 Rom 12:1.
85 *Against the Manichaeans* 10.3–9.

is in that sense that Sarapion claims God is relentless.[86]

In discussing Hades, Sarapion also mentions that the προαίρεσις remains incorrupt despite sin. "For free will (προαίρεσις), whether in a state of understanding or in a state of falling, nevertheless has not been

---

86   With regard to this purgative inclusivism, Sarapion finds himself in company not only with Origen, but more importantly with such luminaries as Clement of Alexandria, Gregory of Nyssa, his sister Macrina, Titus of Bostra and possibly with Gregory Nazianzus and Maximus the Confessor, all of whom uphold a position that did not receive condemnation in the relatively detailed fifteen canons of the fifth ecumenical council, despite its condemnation by Justinian's earlier council. For a discussion concerning Gregory of Nyssa, Gregory Nazianzus, Clement of Alexandria, and Origen, see J.R. Sachs, S.J., "Apocatastasis in patristic theology," *Theological Studies* 54:4 (1993) 617–640. In this article, Sachs also mentions the fifth ecumenical council in relation to the earlier council enacted by Justinian. Unfortunately, he fails to note an important distinction between the "provincial council" of 543 and the ecumenical council of 553. The former condemned the teaching of a finite Hell/Hades and the eventual salvation of all, including the Devil and the demons. The latter condemned only the *apokatastasis* that follows from a pre-existence of souls. The fifteen anathemas of 553 tend to parallel the same errors that Sachs notes Gregory of Nyssa eliminated from his reading of Origen. For a helpful discussion concerning the relationship between the 543 synod and the Ecumenical Council of 553, see A. Grillmeier, in collaboration with T. Hainthaler, *Christ in Christian Tradition*, volume 2, part 2, *The Church of Constantinople in the sixth century*, J. Cawte and P. Allen (trans.), (Atlanta 1995). Grillmeier's own presentation of the anathemas from 543 (page 400) and 553 (pages 404–405) demonstrate that Justinian initially convened a synod that condemned in general terms whereas the ecumenical council condemned an *apokatastasis* of a particular system (that of the Origenists in Palestine, the source of which was Evagrius of Pontus). Titus of Bostra, a Christian opponent of Manichaeism, also believed in the eventual salvation of all. See Pedersen, *Demonstrative Proof in Defence of God*. Additionally, it seems possible that Maximus the Confessor, who post-dates the council of 553, believed similarly. See P. Sherwood's introduction in Maximus the Confessor, *The Ascetic Life; Four Centuries on Charity* (Westminster, MD 1955); B.E. Daley, "Apokatastasis and 'honorable silence' in the eschatology of Maximus the confessor," in F. Heinzer and C. von Schönborn (eds), *Maximus Confessor* (Fribourg 1982) 309–339; F. Norris, "Universal salvation in Origen and Maximus," in N.M. De S. Cameron (ed.), *Universalism and the Doctrine of Hell* (Carlisle; Grand Rapids 1992) 35–72. D. Kelley noted that the list of fathers believing in the eventual salvation of all could well include Gregory of Nyssa, Macrina, Gregory Nazianzus, Clement of Alexandria, Ambrose, and Methodius. He also observes that while Augustine strongly disagrees with such a position, he seems to tolerate it. See D. Kelley, "'Apokatastasis' in the early church," *Patristic and Byzantine Review* 9:1 (1990) 71–74. For an overview of the intricacies of personal relationships amongst the participants of the Origenistic controversies, see E. Clark, *The Origenist Controversy: the Cultural Construction of an Early Christian Debate* (Princeton 1990). Many of the sources just given would question (or at least nuance) the metanarrative of later fathers correcting aspects of Origen's teachings (in light of the fact that sixth century Origenism is not the same as Origen's own beliefs). To the degree that one can still hold to it, Sarapion's place within it must be acknowledged, for his presentation of hell's finitude and the correction of free will in both humanity and angelic beings pre-dates Gregory of Nyssa and is devoid of Origenism's errors, such as the pre-existence of souls, the pre-mundane fall, reincarnation and/or transmigration of souls, etc.

released from being reasonable but maintains this [state] incorrupt."[87] In context, Sarapion speaks not simply of human free will, but of the free will of the demons!

The term προαίρεσις carries an importance for Sarapion. In fact, it is the word he uses for free will throughout the treatise. Casey counts fifteen uses of the term in the treatise.[88] As such, Sarapion employs this word in a technical manner, one that bases itself upon Stoicism. For the Stoics, προαίρεσις meant, first and foremost, a "deliberate or moral choice or purpose".[89] Additionally, προαίρεσις can function as an aspect of Stoic psychology, as something people have.[90] John M. Rist provides a brief history of the word, noting that for Aristotle it meant "choice", but that after nearly disappearing from Stoic vocabulary before the Christian era, "in Epictetus ... *prohairesis* is back with a vengeance. The word occurs time and again, but its meaning is rather wider than can be recognised in Aristotle".[91] For Epictetus, "*prohairesis* now appears then as something more than one of the acts of a man *qua* man: it is both the act of a man and the man himself. A man's *prohairesis* are his character".[92]

One should not make the mistake of thinking that Sarapion adheres to an unfiltered Stoic interpretation of this word. For Stoics, one must make correct use of the προαίρεσις (be this understood as part of one's psychology or as decision or both) so as to achieve a dispassionate and willed acceptance of nature/*logos*, or the way things really are.[93] According to Sarapion, on the other hand, "nature (φύσις) does not guide what defines but free will (προαίρεσις)".[94] "For the will of the one who does the deed happens to be the standard (κανών) for the actions."[95] Therefore, the source of sin is free will with the result that

---

87 Ibid., 29.29-31.
88 Casey, *Manichaeans*, 8.
89 Ibid., 81.
90 T. Brennan, "Stoic moral psychology," in B. Inwood (ed.), *The Cambridge Companion to the Stoics*. Cambridge 2003) 292-294.
91 J.M. Rist, "Prohairesis: Proclus, Plotinus, et alii," in O. Reverdin (ed.), *De Jamblique a Proclus* (Geneva 1975) 105.
92 Ibid.
93 See Schofield, "Stoic ethics", 239-246 and Brennan, "Stoic moral psychology", 257-294.
94 *Against the Manichaeans* 25.4-5.
95 Ibid., 15.12. Indeed, it is precisely because of the way in which Sarapion uses προαίρεσις that I have chosen to translate it as "free will". Although some may object that such a translation is anachronistic, I believe the way in which Sarapion handles the term warrants such an interpretation.

evil "recently has come forth from a sickened free will" (ἐκ προαιρέσεως νοσησάσης).⁹⁶ What's more, this sickened free will brings death:

> The Gospel cried, 'Repent, for the Kingdom of Heaven has drawn near'!⁹⁷ It sent this instruction forth to everyone, spoke to those who stumble, addressed those who have fallen, announced to those who were already bound to death, and solicited freedom through a proclamation.⁹⁸

In a treatise that emphasises the role of free will and evil resulting from a sickened free will, to speak of everyone being bound to death and being in need of the Gospel, goes against Stoic philosophy. For Stoics, death is simply an "indifferent" as it is simply a return to the cosmic fire.⁹⁹ Sarapion sees death in more negative terms. Death is a payment for sin—for the fall of a sickened free will. One's προαίρεσις remains incorrupt, or intact, in the sense that it continues to function, but *how* it functions is up to each of us and so, through one's προαίρεσις, one may choose either virtue or vice, a situation that necessitates the salvific work of Christ.¹⁰⁰

---

96 Ibid., 4.14–15.
97 Matt 3:2.
98 *Against the Manichaeans*, 50.21–25.
99 J. Perkins, *The Suffering Self: Pain and Narrative Representation in the Early Christian Era* (London and New York 1994) 83, 93.
100 See Rist, "Prohairesis", 114, where he argues that Gregory of Nyssa upholds a similar position with regard to προαίρεσις, since "man can choose what *pleases* him ... either for good or for evil." It is also worth noting that the two-fold meaning of προαίρεσις anticipates the distinction St. Maximus the Confessor will later make between "gnomic will" (which is the personal employment of one's will) and "natural will" (which is the human characteristic known as willing). Although Sarapion certainly does not make any such formal distinction, his dual understanding of προαίρεσις assumes a similar distinction. For a succinct description of "gnomic" will, see P. Allen and B. Neil, *Maximus the Confessor and his Companions: Documents from Exile* (Oxford 2003) 16. For discussions concerning free will in Maximus the Confessor's writings, see A. Louth, *Maximus Confessor* (London 1996); J.P. Farrell, *Free Choice in St. Maximus the Confessor* (South Canaan, PA 1989) and *The Disputation with Pyrrhus of our Father Among the Saints Maximus the Confessor* trans. J.P. Farrell (South Canaan, PA 1990). In this way, Sarapion also assumes some sort of a distinction between "person" and "nature". He also assumes that one's free will, one's προαίρεσις may be active even when all the options for choosing are "good". Otherwise, it makes no sense to speak of free will and a purgative, inclusivistic salvation at the same time. The actions of Christ have re-oriented humanity's προαίρεσις so that it is pulled out of Hades and directed toward God, but each person must yet employ his or her προαίρεσις in that direction. In fact, it would seem that Sarapion assumes the dialectical choice between virtue and vice is itself a result of the fall. For discussions on how this is certainly the case for Maximus the Confessor, see the aforementioned works by Farrell and Louth as well as L. Thunberg, *Microcosm and Mediator: The Theological Anthropology of Maximus the Confessor* (Chicago and Lasalle 1995) 144–168.

In addition to προαίρεσις, two other terms should be discussed: ἀρετή (virtue) and ῥᾳθυμία (heedlessness). In the case of the former, Sarapion's Stoic influences shine through. In the case of the latter, Sarapion displays originality on his part. Although ῥᾳθυμία may be used by Stoic philosophers, Sarapion uses it where one might expect ἀφροσύνη (imprudence).

Zeno defined virtue as "reason consistent and firm and unchangeable".[101] Additionally, the final good was connected directly to virtue, in part because virtue measured one's progress toward the final good. "If we take the final good to be unconnected with virtue, we measure the final good by our own advantage, and not by rightness (*honestas*)."[102] Of course, for the Stoics, "to live in accordance with virtue ... is to live in accordance with human nature, and to live in accordance with the requirements of correct reason".[103] Because they are in accordance with nature, virtues are not relative in the sense of a purely situational ethic (though at times, Stoicism does tend in that direction with its discussion of *adiaphora*). "When a man has an attack of vertigo (σκοτωθῇ), it is not the arts and the virtues (αἱ ἀρεταί) that are thrown into confusion (συγχέονται), but the spirit in which they exist."[104] In fact, one should appropriately suffer through hardships because that is precisely how one attains virtue. "He took pride in his distress (περιστάσεσι)...Why, what will he blame God *for*? Because he is living a decent life? What charge does he bring against Him? The charge that He is exhibiting his virtue (ἐπιδείκνυται τὴν ἀρετὴν ἑαυτοῦ) in a more brilliant style?"[105]

Casey notes that virtue (ἀρετή) occurs seventeen times.[106] In each case, Sarapion either uses it in a general sense, such as when he writes, "if self-control (σωφροσύνη) is a virtue (ἀρετή)",[107] or in a more Stoic sense, such as when he speaks of St. Paul at the end of section fourteen:

---

101 Schofield, "Stoic ethics", 241. Schofield cites Plutarch, Chrysippus, and Ariston of Chios, since we do not actually have Zeno's own definition extant, but must rely upon what these three claim his definition was.
102 T.H. Irwin, "Stoic naturalism and its critics," in *The Cambridge Companion to the Stoics*, 348.
103 Ibid., 347.
104 Epictetus, *Discourses*, 3.3.22.
105 Ibid., 3.22.59. In this illustration, Epictetus posited a man suffering from a fever.
106 Casey, *Manichaeans*, 10.
107 *Against the Manichaeans*, 5.3.

> He is the one who has enacted the honour of the new life because he has passed through so many disparaging things (τοσαύτης φαυλότητος), has ascended to such a great height of virtue (ἐπὶ τηλικαύτην ἀκρώρειαν τῆς ἀρετῆς ἀνελήλυθε) and cried, 'For this Jesus Christ came into the world: to save sinners, of whom I am first. Because of this I received mercy, in order that Jesus might exhibit, in me, his entire forebearance (ἅπασαν αὐτοῦ μακροθυμίαν) as an example for those who will believe.'[108]

Sarapion exalts Paul as being the one who displays the new life, something he can do because he has passed through so many hardships and has attained to a great height of virtue. Even the choice of the quotation from Paul resonates with Stoic echoes, as Paul speaks of being someone in whom Jesus has exhibited his own "entire forbearance".

Sarapion applies this Stoic approach to his rebuttal of Manichaean dualism, which would denigrate the body and matter. "Thus the body (and each part) honours the action and imitates the action. What has been made is beautiful (καλόν), for it is able to serve virtue (δύναται γὰρ ὑπηρετῆσαι ἀρετῇ)."[109] Or again:

> O what unprecedented wonder! The sins of saints have been written in order that the truth might be made known, because having produced from similar natures and, in like manner, having produced by means of virtue (ἀρετῇ), they received what is greater, not having prevailed (νικήσαντες) by means of nature (φύσει), but having become prominent (διαπρέψαντες) through virtue (ἀρετῇ).[110]

In this passage, Sarapion attacks the moral implication of dualism and claims that the sins of the saints (especially the failings of the Apostle Peter) demonstrate that it is not nature (as a system with two naturally opposed causes would seem to suggest) but the acquirement of virtue that testifies to someone having prevailed and become prominent in the faith. Sarapion's employment of "virtue" exhibits a use of a Stoic

---

108 Ibid., 14.11–16. 1 Tim 1:15.
109 Ibid., 18.17–19.
110 Ibid., 25.1–4.

approach in the service of a Christian argument against cosmic dualism.

With regard to heedlessness, or ῥᾳθυμία, Sarapion proves even more interesting. Heedlessness, or carelessness, may hinder one's progress toward self-control, one of the four major Stoic virtues (although imprudence, or folly, (ἀφροσύνη) would actually be the corresponding vice). Epictetus presents heedlessness as something that can prevent further progress in virtue: "If you are now neglectful and easy-going (ῥᾳθυμήσῃς), and always making one delay after another, after which you will pay attention to yourself, then without realizing it you will make no progress."[111]

It is worth noting that Sarapion uses the word frequently in *Against the Manichaeans* (although Casey fails to include heedlessness, whether in noun or verbal form, in his list of Sarapion's characteristic words). Heedlessness may be found in sections 7, 8, 12, 13, 17, 18, 19, 46, and 53. In *Against the Manichaeans*, Sarapion develops this vice to a level beyond that found in Stoic writings. Even though he clearly knows of the four vices and four virtues, he elevates heedlessness to the point of being a polar opposite of self-control. When discussing the moral implications for Manichaean dualism in the opening of section 7, he says, "If some of the bodies always were self-controlled (ἐσωφρόνει), not ever heedless (ἐρρᾳθυμηκότα), but some were always heedless (ἐρρᾳθύμει), not restrained by self-control (σωφροσύνη) even in part, it could be said that a division had occurred among the bodies and some were produced self-controlled and some heedless."[112]

What is more, Sarapion goes so far as to link heedlessness to the Fall!

> Therefore, thanksgiving is due to the one who has created our bodies, the one who has providentially cared for the ones who have, themselves, acted heedlessly (ἐρρᾳθυμηκότων). And to the one who sent his own Son in a body and gave it as a pledge for our bodies so that we might no longer bend down and cast our eyes to the ground, but might be straightened through the communion (τῇ κοινωνίᾳ) of the bodies.[113]

---

111 Epictetus, *Encheiridion*, 51.1–2.
112 *Against the Manichaeans*, 7.1–3.
113 Ibid., 53.31–35.

Humanity remains mired in heedlessness and requires a Saviour, someone capable of taking humanity upon himself and properly orienting humanity to the virtues of God.

The Christological Dimension

Sarapion brings both his hermeneutical perspective and his Christianised Stoicism to bear upon his Christology when he addresses the docetic Christology of the Manichaeans. Sarapion writes:

> Yet, he rose from the water, was tried by the Devil, hungered, thirsted, sailed by sea, slept, travelled, grew tired, walked slowly and, being famished, went to the fig tree. Lastly, he suffered, was crucified. What do these facts cry out? What do these things testify? Let tongues be silenced! Let the actions speak! [...] the force of the actions cries out that the Saviour possessed a body, even a mortal body (σῶμα θνητόν), and that he bore (ἐφόρεσε) the body for our sake [...] For in order that he might save his own, he made that one, effecting the freedom of all of his own (πάντων τῶν ἰδίων τὴν ἐλευθερίαν ἐργασάμενος) by making that one.[114]

For Sarapion, the hermeneutical hypothesis, the economies of Christ, demonstrate that Christ possesses a human body and does not exist in a docetic fashion. He "bore" human flesh for our sake. Additionally, Christ came to redeem those who acted heedlessly, that is, to redeem those who lack self-control and proper use of their προαίρεσις.

In light of the evidence of Sarapion's letter exchange with Apollinarius, a brief discussion of the humanity the Son of God encounters is appropriate. Does Sarapion, when arguing against the Manichaeans, adopt a *logos-sarx* approach akin to that of Apollinarius? An important passage necessitates a negative answer to this question. When beginning his discussion of the truly embodied Christ, Sarapion writes:

> For he [Christ] says in the Gospel, 'Whoever looks upon a woman with desire has already committed adultery in his

---

114 Ibid., 53.16–20, 25–26, 30–31.

heart.'[115] And so he attributes the passion (πάθος) in the body to the heart and, in that he concerns himself with seeing, he makes it a common concern with the heart, having introduced the passion (πάθος) of the act of seeing as a passion of the heart, placing concern for the eyes together with a concern for the act of thinking. For the eye does harm in no other way than how the mind does harm. For the eye cannot be perverted (διαστρέφεσθαι) unless the soul is perverted (διαστρέφεσθαι). For when the soul is reasonable and seeing straight, the eyes will also see suitably. So then, having despised the wicked sight, he introduces (παρεισάγει) holy sight so that 'the eyes may see straight and the eyelids might beckon toward righteous things.'[116] For he lifts up the eyes, not allowing them to be guided by themselves, but arousing them and exciting them and preparing them for exalting themselves. So having a great concern (πολλὴν ἐπιμέλειαν) for bodies, he has both borne (πεφόρηκε) a body and entered (ἦλθεν) a body.[117]

Although Sarapion speaks here of the Son bearing a body and entering a body, the link between the soul and body remains important. The body does not sin unless there is a sickness in the soul (a position consistent with claiming that evil arises from a sick προαίρεσις). The sickness that is in need of healing resides not in the body alone. Indeed, a passion of the body may be said to be a passion of the soul. This hardly correlates with what we know of Apollinarius' teaching.[118]

---

115 Matt 5:28
116 Prov 4:25.
117 *Against the Manichaeans* 52.31-42.
118 I am assuming, here, the typical teaching attributed to Apollinarius, that Apollinarius believed the Word replaced the rational soul, or mind, such that Christ had a human body, but not a human rational soul or mind. For a nuanced discussion that speaks of the shifting focus of recent scholarship on Apollinarius and also helps further that shift, see J. Behr, *The Nicene Faith*, part 2 (Crestwood, NY 2004) 377-401. Behr claims: "The most serious problem concerning Apollinarius' account of Christ is not simply his claim that Christ did not assume a human soul or mind, but whether there remains any point of contact between Christ and us: 'He is not a man, but like a man, for he is not consubstantial with man in the highest dimension'" (399). For an extended refutation of Apollinarius, see Gregory of Nyssa's treatise in Friedrich Mueller (ed.), *Gregorii Nysseni Opera* vol. 3 (Leiden 1958) 131-233.

Concluding Remarks: Free Will, Hermeneutics, and Augustine
The hermeneutical and Stoic-ethical approaches form the two central tiers upon which Sarapion builds his case against the Manichaeans. Through his hermeneutic, where the hypothesis of the Lord's economies are found in Scripture and in the oracles proclaiming the Scriptural message, Sarapion refutes the Manichaean rejection of the Old Testament. However, Sarapion also links this discussion to one of virtue and vice, where free will, or προαίρεσις, plays a central role. Although borrowing from Stoicism in this regard, Sarapion also transforms the concept of προαίρεσις. We do not choose to act in accordance with nature, which does not direct us, but we choose, through our free will, to conform to God through virtue or to struggle against him through vice.

However, God sends his Word, who takes upon himself the humanity of all and opens salvation to all. In fact, the eventual salvation of all becomes inevitable, not because angels and people lack free will, but precisely because they have free will. For the προαίρεσις always remains intact and because our faculty of will so remains intact, we cannot eternally choose to defy God. To do that, would be to corrupt, finally and fully, the προαίρεσις. As long as one's προαίρεσις remains intact, God can shape and correct it, for one may be corrected and shaped over time without being "forced". There is no endless, sempiternal dualism opposing God, for Hades, death, and sinfulness all derive from the same source—a use of one's προαίρεσις in opposition to God.[119]

In light of the hermeneutical thrust of the treatise, a brief discussion concerning previous attempts to label Sarapion proves appropriate. While Sarapion has not received extensive attention, especially with regard to discussion concerning an Alexandrine/Antiochene distinction, a few scholars have put forth opinions concerning Sarapion's biblical interpretation. Specifically, R.P. Casey, Maxine West, and Charles Kannengiesser have briefly discussed Sarapion's hermeneutics.

Robert Pierce Casey, reflecting primarily upon Sarapion's *Against the Manichaeans*, though he speaks to the *Letter to the Monks* and the *Letter to Bishop Eudoxius* in the same text, claims:

---

119 For a similar (though much more extensive) reflection upon Gregory of Nyssa, see D.B. Hart, *The Beauty of the Infinite: the Aesthetics of Christian Truth* (Grand Rapids 2003), especially pages 206–207, 272, and 348.

> His [Sarapion's] style and literary manner, his inclination toward philosophical discussion and his evident familiarity with contemporary philosophical ideas are all marks of an educated Greek. In this respect he is closely allied to the older generation of the Catechetical School, Pantaenus, Clement, and Origen [...] On the other hand he was one of the inner circle of Anthony's disciples, and this has also contributed substantially to his development in his admiration for asceticism and in that, unlike Clement and Origen, he has no taste for allegorising Scripture. His exegesis amounts to little more than the application of texts to dogmatic theses and although this is not carried out with the same breadth and rigor as in Athanasius' dogmatic works, [...] it is none the less significant of the change in theological method since the days of Origen. [...] Serapion has a much simpler view of Scripture. The Bible is indeed spiritual, but only in the sense that it is inspired by the Spirit of God and that the reading of it removes all evil from the mind and leads to a veritable conversation with God.[120]

Maxine West follows Casey on this point when discussing the use of the Law in Sarapion's Against the Manichaeans. However, she does so with more charity. "For the most part he [Sarapion] has been logical and thorough, but especially he has explained the psychological benefit words from the law can bring with precision and conviction."[121]

By way of contrast, Charles Kannengiesser places Sarapion within the "Origenian Legacy" in terms of hermeneutic.[122] The puzzling aspect to this, however, is that he provides only a very brief treatment of Sarapion, leaving the reader with only one significant clue as to his reasoning on the matter. He states:

> He [Sarapion] refutes the dualism evident in their [the Manichaeans'] exegesis of the OT and parts of the NT.

---

120 Casey, *Manichaeans*, 23.
121 M. West, "The law, a holy school, Serapion of Thmuis and scripture," in *Studia Patristica: Papers Delivered at the International Conference on Patristic Studies*, Vol. 35 (Louvain 2001) 201.
122 C. Kannengiesser, *Handbook of Patristic Exegesis: The Bible in Ancient Christianity*, Volume 2, (Leiden 2004) 729–730.

Among fragments of other writings (CPG II, 2488–2494), note a few lines from a *Commentary on Genesis* in which the *arche* ("principle," "beginning") of Gn 1:7 is identified with Christ according to Col 1:16 (Devreesse, 104).[123]

Interpreting Genesis with a specific reference to Christ as the beginning, or *arche*, places Sarapion (according to Kannengiesser) within the Origenist school.

The situation placed before the reader of Sarapion's texts, with regard to his hermeneutics, is varied. According to Casey, Sarapion would seem to recall a more simplistic, monastic approach to interpretation, one that was eventually surpassed in the fourth century by more systematic approaches. West presents a similar perspective, though adding that Sarapion is logical and thorough, perhaps meaning Sarapion would be an example of someone who was undergoing the fourth-century shift. His hermeneutic is direct and simple, yet logically and, in this sense, systematically, undertaken. Kannengiesser, following up on Devreesse and a fragment from Sarapion's *Commentary on Genesis*, considers Sarapion to follow the "Origenian Legacy".

Because Sarapion combines Stoic concerns with his hermeneutical thrust, it might seem that his biblical interpretation simply serves to show that the Law (and moral precepts in the Bible as whole) serves to combat the vices and produce virtue, emphasizing the "psychological benefits" or that he provides "little more than the application of texts to dogmatic theses". However, Kannengiesser's insight, though based on a few fragments from Sarapion's commentary on Genesis, proves much more accurate.

In fact, in light of Frances Young's work, Kannengiesser must certainly be more correct than either Casey or West. Frances Young argues that the typical distinction between Alexandria and Antioch is "inadequate" and, in fact, distinguishing "between typology and allegory in early Christian literature is impossible."[124] Young realises that her work

---

123 Ibid., 730. Devreesse, *Les anciens commentateurs grecs*, 104.
124 F. Young, *Biblical Exegesis and the Formation of Christian Culture* (Cambridge 1997), 2. She goes on to reaffirm her position here in "Alexandrian and Antiochian exegesis," in A.J. Hauser and D.F. Watson (eds), *A History of Biblical Interpretation*, vol. 1, *The Ancient Period* (Grand Rapids, MI 2003) 337.

undoes work by significant contributors in the field of early Christian interpretation.[125] Instead of an allegory/history debate, Young argues that the difference was one of rhetoric. She notes that the Antiochenes did not concern themselves with "history", especially history as we would understand it, but with "narrative coherence" and "moral and dogmatic" interpretations.[126] They were also concerned with prophecy and Providence.[127]

According to Young, "Allegory, in its rhetorical usage was a figure of speech among other figures of speech: it was to speak so as to imply something other than what is said, and included irony".[128] The real difference, therefore, between the Alexandrians and Antiochenes, had to do with differing uses of *mimēsis*, or a performance of an epic or drama that creates a representation of life from which the audience may learn.[129] And so, the schools disagreed by way of "a distinction between ikonic and symbolic *mimēsis*" where the former reflects Antiochene exegesis and the latter Alexandrian.[130] Therefore, the Antiochene exe-

---

125 She cites, among others, J. Daniélou, *Origène*, trans. W. Mitchell (New York 1955); *The Lord of History*, trans. Nigel Abercrombie (London 1958); *From Shadows to Reality: Studies in the Biblical Typology of the Fathers* (London 1960); G.W.H. Lampe and K.J. Woollcombe, *Essays in Typology* SBT 22 (London 1957); R.M. Grant and D. Tracy, *A Short History of the Interpretation of the Bible*, 2nd ed. (London 1984); M. Simonetti, *Biblical Interpretation in the Early Church: An Historical Introduction to Patristic Exegesis*, trans J.A. Hughes (Edinburgh 1994); J.N. Guinot, "La typologie comme technique herméneutique," in *Figures de L'Ancien Testament chez les Pères*, Cahiers de *Biblia Patristica* 2 (Strasbourg 1989) 1–34; R.A. Greer, *Theodore of Mopsuestia: Exegete and Theologian* (Westminster 1961), *The Captain of our Salvation: A Study of the Patristic Exegesis of Hebrews* (Tubingen 1973); J.L. Kugel and R.A. Greer, *Early Biblical Interpretation* (Philadelphia 1986); M.F. Wiles, "Origen as biblical scholar," in P. Ackroyd and C.F. Evans (eds), *The Cambridge History of the Bible* (Cambridge 1970); "Theodore of Mopsuestia as representative of the Antiochene school," in P. Ackroyd and C.F. Evans (eds), *The Cambridge History of the Bible*,(Cambridge 1970). She also takes care to note that "typology" is not a patristic term, but a modern one, citing A.C. Charity, *Events and Their Afterlife: The Dialectics of Christian Typology in the Bible* (Cambridge 1966).
126 Young, *Biblical Exegesis*, 163, 297.
127 Ibid., 168. She would later reiterate this point, arguing that both schools shared the same "techniques and assumptions," thus that the Antiochenes' concerns were not with history in a modern sense but with providence and prophecy. See "Alexandrian and Antiochene exegesis", 341, 343.
128 Ibid., 120. See also page 176, where Young provides the same definition based upon the etymology of the word ἀλληγορία, being derived from the Greek verb meaning "to speak in public" and the adjective ἄλλος, or "other."
129 Ibid., 209.
130 Ibid., 162. As Young later states, the Antiochenes simply "rooted their higher sense in a different figure of speech from the *allegoria* of Origen". See "Alexandrian and Antiochene exegesis," 349.

getes preferred to maintain not some sort of literal and/or historical approach, as most all modern scholars have thought, but the overarching narrative of creation, fall, and redemption.[131] Both typology and allegory exist as types of *mimētic* exegesis, yet they are distinct as well. The distinction between the schools parallels that found in the difference between a philosophical reading (as adopted by Alexandrians) and a rhetorical reading (as adopted by Antiochenes).[132]

Even more important for our discussion here is a difference Young fails to note properly, the different approach to a hypothesis. For, she claims that for Irenaeus and Athanasius, hypothesis refers to the rule/canon of faith/truth and, therefore, to the overarching christological reading of the Bible itself.[133] However, she presents hypothesis as meaning the supposed subject matter of a pericope or specific portion of text (such as a Psalm) for the Antiochenes.[134] While she does not draw this out, clearly this must also be a distinguishing feature between Alexandrians and Antiochenes.

Therefore, Sarapion's emphasis upon a hypothesis (the economies of Christ) for the entire Bible, places him within the "Alexandrine" tradition, making Kannengiesser's observation accurate, since understanding Christ to be the *arche* in Genesis 1:7 (because of Colossians 1:16) coheres well with an approach that envisions a christological hypothesis for the whole of the Bible. Sarapion's emphasis on "moral and dogmatic" interpretation might seem to suggest an Antiochene approach, which could cohere better with the conclusions of Casey and West. However, Sarapion clearly upholds a consistency between the Scriptures and the oracles based upon a christological hypothesis. If his emphasis on moral and dogmatic interpretations confuses the picture, then the case of Sarapion suggests that either the "Alexandrine" position needs to be reconsidered so that it allows for any emphasis (from the "loosest" allegory to the "strictest" literalism), so long as it coheres with a christological hypothesis for the entire Christian Bible, or the whole dichotomy between Alexandrine and Antiochene inter-

---

131   Ibid., 296.
132   Ibid., 211.
133   Ibid., 21, 290.
134   Ibid., 171.

pretation needs to be jettisoned and thought of more along the lines of nuance and distinction than opposition and dichotomy (which would be, after all, the direction to which Young points).

In addition to his critical remarks concerning Sarapion's biblical interpretation, Casey also criticises Sarapion for not achieving the type of reflection on Manichaeism and the problem of evil that one reads in Augustine's writings. According to Casey, Sarapion demonstrates a failure to express any

> trace of the specifically Christian theory of evil and its solution through grace [...] Manicheeism, like Pauline and Augustinian Christianity, was not a dialectical approach to the problem of evil, but a strenuous attempt to find a complete solution, theoretical and practical, to a difficulty which was not merely viewed from the outside but felt as a raging within.[135]

Apparently, Sarapion views the problem of evil as an outside observer and thus fails to express a Christian theory based upon grace.

Klaus Fitschen picks up on this critique from Casey and mitigates it. Fitschen considers Sarapion to have provided a complete refutation of Manichaean doctrine.[136] Certainly, by responding to dualism from an ethical perspective and by responding to the Manichaean rejection of the Scriptures, Sarapion refutes the cornerstones of Manichaean doctrine. Fitschen notes that in the midst of this refutation, in 24.3–6 of the treatise, Sarapion explicitly addresses the conflict between good and evil by reminding the reader of the need to be vigilant while referring to 1 Corinthians 9:27.[137] The relevant passage reads as:

> Therefore, I am afraid lest we might not be persuaded. We always toil against something careless (ἀμέλει) so that we might not unexpectedly fall into ruin through carelessness (ἀμέλειαν), thinking we are secure. For our sake, Paul says, "I punish and enslave my body so that, having proclaimed

---

135 Casey, *Manichaeans*, 21. Another aspect to a supposedly Pauline model that Sarapion does not express would be "a pessimistic view of human nature" since Sarapion believes "nature good" but "dictated by an unhealthy will" (20).
136 Fitschen, *Serapion*, 7.
137 Ibid., 52.

to others, I might never become reprobate myself."¹³⁸ I fear this saying regarding reprobation. Knowing the slipperiness of free will (τὸ ὀλισθηρὸν τῆς προαιρέσεως), I secure myself (ἀσφαλίζομαι) against something easy through carefulness (τῇ ἐπιμελείᾳ). I fortify the laxity of free will by the suffering toil of care (τειχίζω τὸ τῆς προαιρέσεως εὐμαρὲς τῷ τόνῳ τῆς μελέτης).¹³⁹

In this passage, Sarapion definitely considers the struggle between good and evil to be a real conflict and one with existential concerns that one could rightfully label as a "raging within." Fitschen also notes that we need to remember that Sarapion did not confront Pelagianism and writes "to what extent he [Sarapion] is surpassed by Augustine, is a question that we must leave open here".¹⁴⁰

The comment concerning Pelagianism cuts to heart of Casey's concern as well. Fitschen demonstrates that Sarapion considers the struggle between good and evil to be a live issue, one that has real existential import, and does not address the issue from the outside as though it is a purely academic question. However, both men seem to assume that the truest, most developed answer to the problem of evil is, necessarily, Augustinian. Although Fitschen does not define explicitly what he understands Augustine to say, Casey provides some defining characteristics. First, as seen above, it must be based upon a concept of "grace". Additionally, Casey claims that the "Pauline" model that Augustine expresses requires "a pessimistic view of human nature", something Sarapion does not express since he believes "nature to be good" but "dictated by an unhealthy will".¹⁴¹ It would seem that Casey means to claim that human nature is not only fallen, but its capacity for free will has been completely destroyed, resulting in a human nature that cannot be termed "good" (at least not in its postlapsarian state).

Because Casey and Fitschen are so indebted to a particular interpretation of Pauline-Augustinian theology, they fail to appreciate fully Sarapion's own argumentation. As noted above, humanity has fallen.

---

138 1 Cor 9:27.
139 *Against the Manichaeans*, 24.1–6.
140 Fitschen, *Serapion*, 53.
141 Casey, *Manichaeans*, 20.

Death and the struggle against heedlessness are the price to be paid. Furthermore, the incarnation acts as the means of grace whereby Christ saves humanity from this state of being.

The struggle with heedlessness exists, necessarily, as a "raging within," but because of the incarnation, this raging within cannot result in a perpetual dualism. God allows for no eternally opposing violence since there is nothing that is not already his. Through the "tortures" of Hades, God "corrects" each rational being, something that can only be done because of the salvific work of Christ, who distils salvation through a "communion" with our bodies. The προαίρεσις does not cease to exist. The capacity for free will remains despite the fall, but this does not eliminate the need for God's grace.

In fact, it is precisely because the προαίρεσις does not cease to exist and God's grace necessarily redeems creation that Sarapion can argue so forcefully against the dualism of the Manichaeans. No form of dualism has the final word. Hades cannot serve as an objective counterpart to God's kingdom. To speak of it in aesthetic terms, when Christ enters a person:

> immediately he draws up the mind, excites the soul, and makes it something uplifted towards better things. Certainly, when someone sees that, he no longer looks to himself but is amazed by the beauty beheld (τῷ θεωρηθέντι κάλλει).[142]

Christ exposes the mind to divine beauty, a beauty that draws one out of his/her struggle with heedlessness and into the sublimity of divinity. Hades, then, serves not as a part of this beauty (for how can the truly beautiful include sempiternal, dualistic violence?) but as a means to correct the false trajectories of the evil uses of our προαίρεσις. To state it again, the salvation of all occurs not because we have no free will, but because our faculty of will remains intact, allowing for God's corrections to shape it. Therefore, Sarapion provides a defence against dualism without falling into either Pelagianism or Fitschen's and Casey's understanding of Augustinian theology.

---

142 *Against the Manichaeans*, 53.59–62.

The *Letter to Bishop Eudoxius*

In this short letter, Sarapion addresses Eudoxius, an otherwise unknown bishop who was suffering through some sort of severe illness at the time. Sarapion provides Eudoxius with the following advice:

> Do not lose heart in suffering (μὴ ἀθύμει πάσχων), but take heart in believing. And do not fall down (κατάπιπτε) when sick, but maintain your powers (εὐτόνει) by not sinning. Do not consider sickness grievous (χαλεπήν). Sin alone is grievous (χαλεπή).
> For, falling ill is common to both good and evil men. But we see that sinning is something peculiar to base men. And the one who is ill has a sickness that ends with his death. But the one who has sinned will find that even after his funeral the sin is still there. [...] Sin lurks and hides in the living, but clings even more to those who have died, and shows its fiery nature[143] and avenges itself on the one who has sinned.
> I have written these things to you, my most longed-for brother so that you do not altogether lose heart but keep yourself in Christ. It is necessary to bear the confusions of life and fitting to endure its tumults (τοῦ βίου τὰς συγχύσεις φέρειν δεῖ, καὶ τοὺς θορύβους βαστάζειν προσήκει) and look to the goal (καὶ πρὸς τὸ τέλος βλέπειν) and know that God presides. [...] Therefore, display the state of your virtue (τῆς σῆς οὖν ἀρετῆς τὴν διάθεσιν δείκνυε) to the all-seeing God, in order that you might be of good repute in all things.[144]

Clearly, Sarapion expresses concern not so much with the illness as with sin.

Fitschen, when discussing this letter, notes that "the basic notion of consolation seems Stoic: illness and death are nothing of concern to us; it applies in retaining—as it is called in the second part of the letter—

---

143 Literally, "flame," (φλόγα).
144 PG 40, 924C-925B.

the virtue in them".[145] Fitschen most certainly must be correct in suggesting a Stoic (even if Christian) context to this advice. Eudoxius is not to consider sickness grievous. That is, he should not apply a moral connotation to the sickness *qua* sickness. The sickness is not the concern, but rather the state of Eudoxius' virtue and sin. Prominent as well is the theme of enduring hardships and concentrating on the goal, or *telos*.

Even the notion of sin producing a flame in the deceased echoes Stoicism, or at least the Stoic doctrine of "conflagration". Such "conflagration" has been undoubtedly Christianised in this context. There is no hint of recurring cycles through a series of beginnings and conflagrations nor does Sarapion attribute the flame/conflagration to the creative principle of nature, but rather to sin, a position perfectly consistent with his presentation of Hades in *Against the Manichaeans*.[146] Nonetheless, to speak of sin as a flame that burns the person after death, especially in the context of a rather Stoic letter, echoes Stoic notions of conflagration. As in the treatise *Against the Manichaeans*, Sarapion displays Stoic influences.

---

145 Fitschen, *Serapion*, 65.
146 On the one hand, it should be noted that Stoics themselves did not all agree on whether the theory of conflagration should be upheld. However, the other alternative was to uphold the notion of an eternal cosmos, along Aristotelian lines. Sarapion's position here echoes conflagration theory, but differs both by making no reference to recurring cosmic cycles (suggesting that the conflagration itself serves to bring humanity closer to its *telos*) and by attributing the fire to human sin rather than to the creative principle of God. For a brief mention of the two different Stoic positions vis-à-vis conflagration, see D. Sedley, "The school, from Zeno to Arius Didymus," in *Cambridge Companion to the Stoics*, 23-24. For a discussion concerning fire as a creative principle of God, such that the conflagration dissolves all things but then creates anew, see M.J. White, "Stoic natural philosophy [physics and cosmology]," in *The Cambridge Companion to the Stoics*, 129-130, 133-138, 141-143.

The Letter to the Monks and the *Adiaphora* of the World

In the *Letter to the Monks*,[147] Sarapion again displays his indebtedness to Stoic philosophy and a hermeneutic consistent with *Against the Manichaeans*. He also exhibits indebtedness to his Egyptian religious milieu. In this letter, he places suffering and hardships within a Christianised Stoic context, whereby suffering entails the acquirement of virtue and can foster salvation. One can detect Sarapion's indebtedness to Stoicism in the *Letter to the Monks* in two ways: through a discussion of worldly things that cohere with viewing them as "*adiaphora*" and through his use of some key terms. Taken together, a Stoic influence seems impossible to deny. One central theme is that Sarapion presents the monks to whom he is writing as Stoic *proficientes*, those who fulfil a role just below that of the true sage but who have advanced well beyond the rest of humanity. With respect to the hermeneutic used in the letter, Sarapion presents a biblical interpretation consistent with that given above for *Against the Manichaeans*, though with a twist. The monastic life produces a *lived* Christocentric interpretation. Sarapion displays his indebtedness to his Egyptian, religious milieu by adding a unique role to the ascetic undertaking of monks: they fulfil a role Egyptians had previously ascribed to the Pharaoh and one that the author of the *Apocalypse of Elijah* had ascribed to Christian martyrs not very long before Sarapion.

Although the notion of a monastic text speaking about renouncing worldly things and activities may strike us as trite and hardly "Stoic," it is worth remembering that when this letter was written, monasticism was still in its early flowering, a development that occurred in a Graeco-Roman context. More importantly, an examination of the things Sarapion dismisses, and the way in which he does so, results in language that resonates with Stoic emphases.

Near the opening of the treatise, Sarapion exclaims:

---

147 Translated from PG 40, 925–941.

> You were not seduced by human reasoning (ἀνθρωπίνοις λογισμοῖς) nor have the things of life that seem desirable (ποθεινά) been able to lessen (ἐλαττῶσαι) the intensity of your desire (πόθου) for God. But in general, having been set apart in all things, you have one aim—to please God.[148]

In fact, he says later:

> You are free (ἐλεύθεροί ἐστε) in all things, oh monks, most divinely favoured by God! A wife does not trouble (ἐνοχλεῖ) you concerning womanly adornments. Sons or daughters are not harassing (συμπνίγουσι) you by bringing disagreeable (διαφόρους) requests to you. Nor does a servant, after stealing valuables, run away. Nor does a concern about wealth (χρημάτων μέριμνα) steal your sleep.[149]

This renunciation of wealth and worldly pursuits and even family life recurs throughout the letter.

The citations just given provide enough material to begin considering a Stoic background. On a general level, Stoic psychology held that

> among the utterly wicked [...] most impulses are emotional—people act with the sincere though misguided thought that life, health, and money are good things, and they fear death, disease, and poverty as bad things.[150]

More precisely, Epictetus notes the dangers of failing to care for the one important thing (attaining to a dispassioned, willed acceptance of nature or the *logos*, whereby we come to see things as God sees them) by caring for the distractions of life:

> But now, although it is in our power to care (ἐπιμελεῖσθαι) for one thing only and devote ourselves to but one, we choose rather to care (ἐπιμελεῖσθαι) for many things, and to be tied fast to many, even to our body (σώματι) and our estate (κτήσει) and brother (ἀδελφῷ) and friend (φίλῳ) and child (τέκνῳ) and slave (δούλῳ). Wherefore, being

---
148 PG 40, 928A.
149 PG 40, 932A–B.
150 Brennan, "Stoic moral psychology," 271.

tied fast to many things, we are burdened (βαρούμεθα) and dragged down (καθελκόμεθα) by them.[151]

Although Epictetus does not mention "wife" specifically, here, she could fall under the category of "estate," and certainly fits within the types of concerns Epictetus raises, including children, slaves, and wealth.[152]

Sarapion also raises the issue of the estate and brothers and friends earlier in his letter, not long after claiming the monks were not seduced by the things of the world. He writes:

> not one impediment (ἐμπόδιον) has been able to hinder (ἐκκόψαι) your heavenly purpose—not a desire for wealth (χρημάτων πόθος), not a memory of parents (μνήμη γονέων), nor family inheritances (πρὸς γένους κληρονομίαι), nor conversations with brothers (ἀδελφῶν συνουσίαι), not a family will (συγγενῶν διαθέσεις), not luxuries (τρυφαί) such as baths and drinking bouts, not the intervention of friends (φίλων συντυχίαι), not the glories of the world (κοσμικαὶ δόξαι), but having despised (ὑπερφρονήσαντες) everything, you cry out against these works, declaring the Apostle's saying, 'I regard all things as refuse (σκύβαλα) in order that I might gain Christ.'[153]

The very sorts of things that Epictetus claims the true (Stoic) philosopher must disregard as distractions, Sarapion regards as distractions or, citing St. Paul on this matter, as "refuse". In each case as well, the men present such distractions as hindering the one important thing that all are called to do. We know that Epictetus (as a Stoic) refers to a dispassionate and willed acceptance of nature/*logos*, or the way things really are. Sarapion's understanding of humanity's *telos* is a life in Christ in the eschaton, something that can be seen below when discussing the ending of his *Letter to the Monks*. Sarapion parallels Epictetus with respect to the renunciation of worldly distractions.

Throughout much of the letter, Sarapion simply expands upon the

---

151 Epictetus, *Discourses* 1.1.14-15.
152 It is also conceivable that the inclusion of "wife" might be a Christian (especially monastic) innovation. However, I have not performed a thorough investigation into this possibility and so I raise it simply for the sake of consideration.
153 PG 40,928C. Phil 3:8.

details of what these distractions bring. In one instance, he even briefly breaks into an exaggerated story of one who chooses to marry and live a city life:

> Whenever someone marries in a city, it is a source of crises, a necessity of expenditures. Is one's wife pregnant? Has she given birth? Has the baby been born? The man's concern will be how he will fulfil all the thoughts of his wife. Is the child born a girl? The man is disgusted (ἀηδίζεται) that he is being robbed concerning the dowry. Was the child born a boy? His countenance is joyful for a short time. Not long after, the child has collapsed from sickness. Being a calamity (συμφορά) for the man, he does not cease calling physicians. He will give many things if the child will be saved. Going to his friends with his eyes cast down, he meets them saying, 'Pray! Because my child is sick. If he should die, I will hang myself'! The friends console (συνέχονται) him. But God provides life for the family's goodwill. The little child gets better, grows, gets taller, and becomes a youth. Various teachers take over this one and as he grows, he is instructed according to the world. He becomes then a young man, suitable for marital union. His father is occupied with marriage. Everything was prepared; the bride-chamber was prepared, but death suddenly snatched away the young man. The unforeseen calamity (συμφορά) is unbearable (ἀνηκέστως) to the father. The young man is buried. Henceforth, there are moanings and lamentations, when the father arrives at the funeral shouting loud lamentations and hitting his head with his hands, shaking and striking his face, while continuously saying, 'Woe is me! Woe is me'! And being very distressed by the calamity (συμφορά), he often falls into serious illness, and being consumed little by little, he henceforth cries out for death.[154]

From a Stoic perspective, it would be difficult to find a more pathetic case. The man so invested himself in the *adiaphora* of life that his son's death was "unbearable" (ἀνηκέστως). He could not endure the pain and

---

154 PG 40,932C–D.

infliction of his son's death and descends into a mire of sickness, calling out for death to take him. The man would have been better off had he followed Epictetus' advice and not bound himself so to his child in the first place.

Sarapion also presents reflections upon two additional themes important to Stoic reflection. John T. Fitzgerald notes that Seneca writes, "exile, the torture of disease, wars, shipwreck—we must think on these"![155] Fitzgerald raises this statement of Seneca in the course of discussing the importance of ascesis for the Stoics. "The training must be total, lest Fortune find a corridor of vulnerability and race through it to the unprotected area."[156] In addition to a story that reflects upon sickness and disease (and death), Sarapion provides brief reflections both upon serving in the army and the perils of a shipwreck.

With respect to war, or at least service in the army, he writes:

> You have not been enrolled in the army (ἐστρατεύθητε) of a human king in order that you might see the slaughter of fellow men in war, but you have been enrolled in the army (ἐστρατεύθητε) of Christ in order that you might see the defeat of demons. Nor do you have weapons of copper and iron to kill fellow servants. Rather, you have acquired a strong faith (ἔκτησθε πίστιν ἰσχυράν) whereby the devil has been overthrown. Furthermore, you have not been enrolled in the army (ἐστρατεύθητε) in order that you might pour out human blood, but you have been enrolled in the army (ἐστρατεύθητε) of God in order that you might continuously pour out your supplication to his face.[157]

With respect to shipwreck, he says, "neither have you feared the sea, that when suddenly aroused by a storm, it might utterly destroy your ship's cargo and you, a rich man, might immediately be found to be a poor man".[158]

---

155 J.T. Fitzgerald, *Cracks in an Earthen Vessel: an Examination of the Catalogues of Hardships in the Corinthian Correspondence* (Atlanta 1986) 92. The reference is to *Ep.* 91.7.
156 Ibid.
157 PG 40,937A-B.
158 PG 40,933B.

Sarapion's description of the perils of a shipwreck coheres not only with Seneca's statement, but also with a passage from Epictetus, where he writes:

> That is why, if the weather keeps us from sailing, we sit down and fidget and keep constantly peering about. 'What wind is blowing?' we ask. Boreas. 'What have we to do with it? When will Zephyrus blow'? When it pleases, good sir, or rather when Aeolus pleases. For God has not made you steward of the winds, but Aeolus. 'What then'? We must make the best of what is under our control (τὰ ἐφ' ἡμῖν), and take the rest as its nature is (τοῖς δ' ἄλλοις χρῆσθαι ὡς πέφυκεν). 'How, then, is its nature'? As God wills (ὡς ἂν ὁ θεὸς θέλῃ).[159]

Epictetus discusses the wind. However, since it follows on the heels of his statements concerning the estate, one can conclude that the real concerns Epictetus implies, Sarapion mentions explicitly.

Sarapion's discussion of war and serving in the army raises a final Stoic theme I wish to highlight—the notion of monks as those who live the life of a *proficiens*.[160] The category of the *proficiens* developed in Stoic thought within the context of debating the existence of the truly wise man, one who without any doubt was a sage of the highest degree. Although the Cynics had held that such a person could exist, milder Stoics, beginning with the Middle Stoa (late second and first centuries BC), developed an understanding of an intermediate person, the *proficiens*, with later Stoics distinguishing three levels of *proficientes*. In discussing this phenomenon, Fitzgerald provides some important insights useful for engaging Sarapion's *Letter to the Monks*:

> The most advanced of the *proficientes* 'have already arrived at a point from which there is no slipping back' into the various faults from which they have escaped. They have gained a place near wisdom and 'have already laid aside all passions and vices'. Yet, decisively, 'their assurance (*fiducia*)

---

159 Epictetus, *Discourses* 1.1.16–17.
160 My entire discussion here, concerning the *proficiens*, is taken from Fitzgerald, *Cracks in an Earthen Vessel*, 56–59.

is not yet tested,' and they do not even realise their impregnable position.¹⁶¹

This description fits exactly the status of the monks to whom Sarapion writes. As already observed in the citations given thus far from the letter, the monks have laid aside the passions and the vices. This becomes heightened near the end of the letter where Sarapion, after discussing the efficacy of the monks' spiritual fathers and the monks themselves, writes:

> You know these things more accurately than we do. For you have spent time with them and so have your fathers. Therefore, who will be able to declare your praises worthily? Who will not approve (ἀποδέξεται) or commend (ἐπαινέσειεν) your love of God, patience, intelligence, and purity, along with your prudence (φρόνιμον), gentleness and silence (ἡσύχιον), civilised manners, peacefulness, absence of pretence, and straightforwardness, dispassion (ἀπαθές), unselfishness, tenderheartedness, compassion, generosity, sympathy, brotherly love and hospitality, love toward beggars, friendliness in conversation, love of truth, single-mindedness (ὁμόνοιαν) with respect to God, your words, sweet as honey, your soft speech, your sure-footedness, solitude (ἀναχώθρησιν), outstanding fame (τὸ χρηστὸν ὄνομα),¹⁶² orthodoxy, and faith in God? [...] Therefore, when anyone remembers you, he also certainly applies praise to you. Therefore, most courageous men (ἀνδρειότατοι), because you clearly acknowledge your dignity and glory, you have prevailed (ἐνισχύσατε) in perfecting your reward by being increasingly vigilant because of the hope of things to come and by singing David's phrase: "Take courage! (Ἀνδρίζου) Let your heart be strengthened and wait on the Lord".¹⁶³

---

161 Fitzgerald, *Cracks in an Earthen Vessel*, 58. The quotations are from Seneca, *Ep.* 75.9.
162 Literally, this speaks of the monks' "good name". I have chosen to highlight the fact that to have a good reputation requires being rather well-known in the first place. This would seem to be yet another occurrence of monks being well-known during their own lifetimes (though not in as specific a manner as Anthony or Poemen since we do not know the addressees of this letter).
163 PG 40,940 C–D, 941A. The biblical citation is Ps 26:14 (27:14).

Clearly the monks have already achieved virtue and have gone beyond passion and vice. For who can declare their praises worthily? The monks have already prevailed in their struggle to attain virtue.

And yet Sarapion ends the letter (following almost immediately after the quotations just given) as follows:

> May some other view never bring all this to ruin (μηδὲ πώποτε κἂν ἔννοιά τις ἐμφωλεύῃ τὸ σύνολον). Nor, after so much time, may some slight heedlessness (ῥᾳθυμια) regarding the things good for your soul extinguish your brilliant lights, a wind blowing in the opposite direction, since you appear as lights of heaven shining in the world, in order that you might hear, together with the apostles, 'You are the light of the world,'[164] and also the Apostle saying, 'You have need of endurance (ὑπομοηῆς), so that having done the will of God, you might honour his promise'.[165]
>
> So, do not grow weary (μὴ ἀποκάμητε), most honoured men, but connect the end to the beginning and the beginning to the end. "For the one who endures to the end (Ὁ γὰρ ὑπομείνας εἰς τέλος)—this one—will be saved."[166] May it come to pass that you and we, who are nourished by divine dogmas, ruled by God, and shepherded by him, attain (τυχεῖν) a blessed and holy end, having been trained for it so that having succeeded (κατορθώσαντας), we might boldly say those prayerful words spoken by the Apostle: "I have fought the good fight. I have completed the race. I have kept the faith. From now on, there is reserved for me a crown of righteousness, which the Lord, the Righteous Judge, will give to me on that day."[167]

---

164 Matt 5:14.
165 Heb 10:36. Migne offers κομίσησθε, the verb also cited in the critical Greek text edited by Aland and others, for κοσμήσησθε, the verb in Sarapion's text. I have chosen to accept the verb given in the text of the letter (κοσμήσησθε). To change it according to what occurs in Aland's text presupposes either that Sarapion cannot testify to a manuscript variant or that he could not have been writing from memory (in this case, at least). For further consideration into the possible uniqueness of Sarapion's biblical citations (especially the New Testament citations), see A. Globe, "Serapion of Thmuis as witness to the Gospel text used by Origen in Caesarea," *Novum Testamentum* 26:2 (1984) 97-127.
166 Matt 24:13.
167 2 Tim 4:7-8.

This is precisely the sort of ending one might expect from a bishop (and monk) to monks whom he considers *proficientes*. They have attained to virtue and surpassed the passions and vices and yet still need to endure. The full and complete testing of their attaining to virtue has not yet occurred. Even the importance placed upon endurance resonates with a Stoic context. As Judith Perkins notes, endurance and forbearance are Stoic "watchwords."[168] For example, for Epictetus, the lecture hall of the philosopher is a hospital, from which students should walk out enduring pain,[169] which is to be expected, given that the philosopher should be judged, in part, on how well he endured.[170]

Stoic Terminology

In addition to such obviously Stoic concepts or themes, and his use of the "watchword" "endurance", Sarapion uses a few other key Stoic terms as well. The letter's brevity and the fact that it is not a strictly philosophical piece of writing (in the sense of a treatise) cautions against making too much of Sarapion's appropriation of words important within a Stoic vocabulary. Nonetheless, the context provided by the use of Stoic themes at least encourages the possibility that a few uses of some key words echo Stoic uses of those same terms. Specifically, Sarapion uses: προαίρεσις (free will/an act of choosing), ῥᾳθυμία (heedlessness/carelessness), ἀνδρεία (courage/manliness), and ἀρετή (virtue).

The word προαίρεσις occurs only once in Sarapion's *Letter to the Monks*, but its occurrence proves significant both for demonstrating further Stoic indebtedness on Sarapion's behalf and in light of the discussion concerning the monks as *proficientes*. The passage is as follows: τῆς ἀποδεκταίας ταύτης καὶ ἀγαθῆς προαιρέσεως ὁ χορηγὸς γενόμενος καὶ ἀρχηγὸς καὶ τελειωτὴς ἔστιν Ἰησοῦς ὁ Χριστός ("the Leader who is both the originator and the accomplisher of this acceptable and good

---

168 Perkins, *The Suffering Self*, 80. Perkins notes that Gellius "reported on Epictetus' understanding of the worst vices: 'a lack of endurance [*intolerantiam*] and a lack of self-control [*incontinentiam*]'".
169 Epictetus, *Discourses*, 3.1.10–11, 3.23.30, 3.23.37.
170 Ibid., 4.8.20, where Epictetus asks people "see how…I endure (ἀνέχομαι)?" while discussing the fact that a philosopher's garb does not make a philosopher. Fitzgerald, *Cracks in an Earthen Vessel*, 72, notes that the endurance of adversity must be rational and voluntary.

way of life is Jesus the Christ").[171] In context, προαίρεσις refers to a course of life, or the conduct of the monks.

Therefore, it may initially seem that a Stoic understanding of προαίρεσις does not apply in this case. However, if we recall the understanding of προαίρεσις given above when discussing its occurrence in *Against the Manichaeans*, where Rist reminds us that προαίρεσις may mean something more along the lines of a disposition resulting from past decisions (and in this sense may be defined as "purpose"), then Sarapion's use of the word here should be interpreted as more Stoic than it might have seemed at first.

Fitzgerald offers a reflection on προαίρεσις that situates Sarapion's usage of this word within the context of the discussion concerning the *proficientes*. "The witness that the sage bears as a paradigm has to do with things which lie outside the realm of the *prohairesis* and it consists in the message that true goods reside within, not in externals."[172] Fitzgerald's observation is significant for our discussion here because if it is the case that the sage, the one who is truly wise, is the one who brings the message concerning the importance of the προαίρεσις, then Sarapion situates himself squarely within the milder Stoic tradition, claiming that the sage is exceedingly rare but the existence of *proficientes* occurs. In fact, according to Sarapion, the sage is so rare that there is only one sage—Jesus the Christ.

Sarapion's use of the word ῥᾳθυμία proves fairly conventional by Stoic standards. As noted above when discussing *Against the Manichaeans*, heedlessness may hinder one's progress in virtue toward self-control. For Sarapion, the relevant passage is: μηδὲ τοῦ τοσούτου χρόνου βραχεῖά τις ῥᾳθυμία τῶν ἀγαθῶν ὑμῶν τῆς ψυχῆς ἐναντίος ἄνεμος πνεύσας σβέσει τὰ λάμποντα φῶτα ("nor, after so much time, may some slight heedlessness toward the things good for your soul extinguish your brilliant lights"). Here, Sarapion simply follows in the footsteps of the Stoics and presents heedlessness as the primary concern for the *proficientes*-monks following the divine sage, Jesus the Christ. Heedlessness may not be the corresponding vice to self-control, but it can prevent growth in virtue toward complete self-control.

---

171 PG 40, 928A.
172 Fitzgerald, *Cracks in an Earthen Vessel*, 81.

Sarapion's use of ἀνδρεία is likewise conventional by Stoic standards. "The ideal philosopher or sage possesses all the virtues, and he uses them all in meeting adversity, whatever its source. Both popularly and historically, however, it is especially ἀνδρεία that is manifested in the midst of hazards and hardships."[173] Epictetus chides those who do not discern their purpose in life, becoming cowardly in light of their situation in life, rather than for "high-mindedness, nobility of character, courage (ἀνδρείας)".[174] As seen above, Sarapion calls the monks ἀνδρειότατοι ("most courageous men") which, perhaps, leads him to cite Psalm 26:14 (LXX): Ἀνδρείζου καὶ κραταιούσθω ἡ καρδία σου καὶ ὑπόμεινον τὸν Κύριον ("Take courage! Let your heart be strengthened and wait on the Lord"). Near the end of the letter, after having discussed all the ascetic hardships the monks endure, Sarapion calls them "most courageous" or "most manly", in perfect conformity with Stoic philosophy.

The monks are so courageous or manly that according to Sarapion (a little earlier in the letter), the monks will be greeted by their admirers, which will include an encounter with Job. "There you will see the most courageous (ἀνδρειότατον) Job, a participant in your sufferings (πόνων) and an admirer of your endurance (ὑπομονῆς), surrounded with many glories."[175] Job, who is already "most courageous" nonetheless admires the monks' endurance, having suffered similar hardships himself. Sarapion simultaneously makes Job an exemplar of the kind of Stoic Christianity Sarapion sees in the monks and makes the monks the examples to which Job himself looks. Courage, or manliness, although employed for Sarapion's Christian purpose, nonetheless accords perfectly well with Stoicism.

Sarapion also uses a synonym of ἀνδρεία, θάρρος. Sarapion tells the monks, "You have firmly renounced the world and its cares, having greatly taken courage (θαρρήσαντες) in the divine saying, 'Seek first the Kingdom of God and his righteousness and all these things will be given to you'".[176] Epictetus actually uses this word for courage in several places, so Sarapion hardly removes himself from a Christianised Stoic

---

173 Ibid., 87.
174 Epictetus, *Discourses*, 4.1.109.
175 PG 40,937C.
176 PG 40,936B. Matt 6:33.

context by means of the synonym θάρρος.[177]

With respect to ἀρετή (virtue), Sarapion uses the term in a manner consistent with Stoicism. Already, we have seen that Sarapion lists virtues the *proficientes*-monks have acquired and that the final good, or the goal (*telos*) is not human nature but the eschaton, where the saints surround the monks and Christ stands at their head, which is why they must continue to endure. Keeping this different understanding of *telos* in mind, one can see that Sarapion uses the virtues to demonstrate the progress the monks have made. If the virtues applied to the monks imply this, then Sarapion makes the point clear. "Oh, with how much virtue (πόσῃ ἀρετῇ) have you lived! Oh, how much virtue (πόσαι ἀρεταί) surrounds you, most honoured men of God! Oh, from how many virtues (πόσων ἀρετῶν) do you wear a crown!"[178] In fact, these lines come immediately upon the heels of the virtues listed in the earlier citation above. The monks demonstrate their progress toward the Kingdom of God through their acquirement of virtue and it is for this reason that they look upon worldly sufferings as *adiaphora* and live through their monastic hardships. If (as noted when discussing virtue in *Against the Manichaeans*) Epictetus' man could virtuously sustain his fever, then Sarapion's monks have surpassed even him, for they not only avoid blaming God, but are living a life in praise and service to him, undertaking the voluntary monastic hardships and acquiring virtue.

The Monks as Spiritual Descendants of Pharaoh

Although the Stoic concepts prominently display themselves throughout Sarapion's *Letter to the Monks*, another aspect comes through as well. The monks serve Egypt in the same manner that the pharaohs of old had. Not too far into the letter, Sarapion breaks into the following praise of the monks:

> You have not cared about worldly love nor the things in this world. Therefore, you are blessed before God and the world is also blessed through you (καὶ ὁ κόσμος δι' ὑμᾶς). The deserts are being exalted through you (σεμνύνονται

---

177 See, for example, Epictetus, *Discourses*, 3.22.96, 3.26.5, 3.26.36.
178 PG 40,940D.

> δι' ὑμᾶς) and the inhabited world is being saved by your prayers (ἡ οἰκουμένη σώζεται ταῖς ὑμετέραις προσευχαῖς). The rain is sent down upon the earth by your supplications, the earth produces green plants, and the trees, laden with fruits, yield undamaged fruit. The river, flooding yearly and watering the whole of Egypt, forming into marshy lakes and distributing a great amount into the sea, makes known the power of your supplications. For if (as it is written)[179] Elijah, who was a passionate man like all others (ἄνθρωπος ἦν ὁμοιπαθής), both held back the rain and restored it again by prayer, and the heavens sent rains and the earth grew her fruit, how much more effective will your intercessions (πρεσβεῖαι) be for gaining advantages (ἀνίσει χρήσιμα) for us by your prayers? Therefore, the city of Alexandria is blessed by having you as mediators (πρεσβευτάς).[180]

Although it might seem that such language is simply further hyperbole on the part of Sarapion toward the *proficientes*-monks, the passage resonates with an indigenous Egyptian religious quality.

David Frankfurter, in discussing the *Apocalypse of Elijah,* provides two passages from that work that parallel the passage above from Sarapion's *Letter to the Monks.* He gives them as following:

> [Immediately after the "saints" are removed from the earth:] Then, in that time, the earth will tremble; the sun will darken. Peace will be removed from upon the earth and under heaven [...] The trees will be uprooted and topple over. Wild beasts and farm animals will die in a catastrophe. Birds will fall on the ground dead, the earth will parch, and the waters of the sea will dry up.
>
> The sinners will lament on the earth, What have you done to us, Lawless One,...See, now we will die in a famine and tribulation....
>
> We went to the depths of the sea
>   And we found no water.

---

179 Jas 5:17-18 and 1 Kgs 17-18, especially 17:1 and 18:40-46.
180 PG 40,929A-B.

> We dug in the rivers and papyrus reeds
> And we found no water. [5:7–10a, 12a, 14 (Sa)]
>
> Bring up the saints—
> For because of them the earth gives fruit,
> For because of them the sun shines upon the earth,
> For because of them the dew falls upon the earth!
> [5:18 (Sa)][181]

Frankfurter notes that the two passages speak of the saints "as an ordering force in the land and the cosmos at large, the cause of fertility and irrigation and the sun", though in the first passage this is implied through portraying what occurs in the saints' absence, while the second passage directly describes the saints' role in the cosmos.[182] Frankfurter observes, "the wide-ranging, integrative functions and powers attributed to the 'saints' are precisely those with which the *Pharaoh* was traditionally idealised in Egyptian tradition down through the Roman period (when such idealizations were all that remained of the kingship).[183] As Silverman notes:

> A ruler envisioned as both human and divine was best suited to intercede between the human and divine worlds. The king functioned as the high priest of every god, making offerings directly to each deity. He thus stood between the god and humankind. [...] When the king ruled, a proper balance was maintained, enabling the ordered universe to persist.[184]

In the *Apocalypse of Elijah*, the "saints" are the martyrs.[185] The bodily

---

181 D. Frankfurter, "The cult of the martyrs in Egypt before Constantine," *Vigiliae Christianae* 48 (1994) 28.
182 Ibid., 29.
183 Ibid.
184 D.P. Silverman, "Divinity and deities in ancient Egypt," in B.E. Shafer (ed.), *Religion in Ancient Egypt: Gods, Myths, and Personal Practice* (Ithaca and London 1991) 64, 67.
185 Ibid. See Frankfurter, "Cult of the martyrs", 31, where he argues that the phrase "bring up the saints" in [5:18 (Sa)] refers to a bodily presence, a conclusion justified in light of the fact that in Egypt "traditional mortuary practice even through the Roman period" included a desire to maintain the physical family including corpses. Furthermore, Frankfurter notes that keeping the physical bodies of the martyrs in the midst of believers was a Melitian practice (31–32). Frankfurter cites Athanasius' *Ep.* 41 concerning Melitian practice.

presence (literally, their relics) of the martyrs preserves the cosmic order of Egypt and the cosmos more generally. In Sarapion's *Letter to the Monks*, the subject producing cosmic orderliness has shifted to the *proficientes*-monks. In this shift, the traditional, Egyptian religious need for a person who intercedes on humanity's behalf has been transformed. According to Sarapion, it is the Christian monks who perform this task, a task once attributed to the pharaohs and later, by the author of the *Apocalypse of Elijah*, to the bodily presence of the deceased martyrs.

As an aside, it may be worth noting that Sarapion might actually be responding to the *Apocalypse of Elijah* in this passage when he writes to the monks. Frankfurter writes:

> One is tempted [...] to view, in such a 'rigorist' [martyriological] milieu as the Apocalypse of Elijah seems to reflect, the ideological and social roots of the Melitians. While not attacking "Alexandrian" ecclesiastical authorities in any explicit way, the Apocalypse of Elijah elsewhere demonstrates ideological tendencies in polemic with those we can reconstruct as Alexandrian.[186]

In Sarapion's letter, the monks explicitly preserve the order of Alexandria. Whether this serves simply to heighten the praise for the monks, who have rallied around Athanasius and Sarapion or whether this passages serves as an implicit correction and/or warning (or both), one cannot definitively say.

Additionally, Sarapion's reference to Elijah in this particular context may also serve a polemical purpose. "Elijah himself was so important as a paradigm and as a source of power for hermits as well as lay people that any text purporting to contain the revelations of Elijah would be met with considerable interest."[187] For the *proficientes*-monks to whom Sarapion writes exceed the powers and prestige of Elijah, implying that it is not they who are subservient to Elijah and in need of his revelation, but Elijah who is subservient to the monks.

---

186 D. Frankfurter, *Elijah in Upper Egypt: The Apocalypse of Elijah and Early Egyptian Christianity* (Minneapolis 1993) 154. He notes the text's millennialism, its homily on rigorous fasting, and its use of traditional anti-Alexandrian oracles as evidence of anti-Alexandrian tendencies.
187 Ibid., 75.

"Suffering" in the Letter to the Monks

With the preceding discussions concerning the Stoic and Egyptian religious contexts in mind, an understanding of suffering can be perceived in the *Letter to the Monks*. Sarapion addresses suffering in two ways in his *Letter to the Monks*. On the one hand, there are the voluntary, monastic hardships that the monks endure. This aspect does not receive much description in the letter though it is present. Primarily, Sarapion implies it through his discussions of endurance and courage. However, he does say to the monks, "you are always content with necessity, being vigorous in fasting, more vigorous in prayer. Vigils are completed in wakefulness by you every day."[188]

In many ways, however, sufferings are to be surpassed. They are activities through which one acquires virtue. Unlike the fictional father who invests too much of himself into the furthering of his estate and his progeny, which leads to the father's mental and physical breakdown, the *proficiens*-monk renounces such things and dismisses them as having no ultimate importance in and of themselves. Hardships serve to produce virtuous character and unlike most people, the monks have transcended the daily sufferings associated with worldly living and embraced the monastic hardships, hardships which lead to further virtue and the life as *proficientes*. The role of these *proficientes*-monks does not revolve around their own concerns for inward purity, but serves to further the good of the entire cosmos. By integrating indigenous Egyptian religious concerns, Sarapion shifts the value of monastic strivings from the relatively self-focused Stoic approach to one that places the concern for others, and indeed all of nature, at the pinnacle of the monastic, ascetic undertaking. In this way, those who transcend the worldly life and its peculiar hardships and sufferings are the very same people who sustain the existence of those who live within those worldly endeavours.

The Hermeneutics of the Letter to the Monks

Although the *Letter to the Monks* and *Against the Manichaeans* exhibit two different genres of writing, Sarapion exhibits a consistency not

---

188 PG 40,929A.

only with regard to the Stoic influences, but also with respect to his biblical interpretation.[189] Because he does not argue against an opposing use (or disregard) for part of the Bible, he does not put forth his position as explicitly as he does in *Against the Manichaeans*. Nonetheless, one can discern continuity between the documents with regard to Christ as the hypothesis for interpreting the Bible. In this letter, however, Sarapion provides a twist to this theme. For him, the monks (at least the ones he addresses) live out this interpretation. Properly exegeting a Christocentric interpretation does not remain an intellectual activity alone, but is to be a way of life, so much so, that that is exactly what monasticism itself is, a Christocentric interpretation of the Bible.

Sarapion demonstrates this perspective from the outset with the first biblical citation in the letter. Its placement, in context, is as follows:

> The Leader who is both the originator and the accomplisher of this acceptable and good way of life is Jesus the Christ. He is also the one who gives to you monks a power to endure and a most worthy end, and who secures, for all those desiring to be saved, an assured course, which you have been eager to travel from the beginning. You have, as a fellow traveller, the Saviour Lord who says, 'I do not neglect you nor abandon you.'[190]

Sarapion opens his treatise with a reference to words from Jesus Himself. However, the phrase in question is actually from Hebrews 13:5, which quotes from Joshua 1:5 (a passage where God assures Joshua that God's presence will be with him). Sarapion's use of this quotation in this manner suggests at least two things. First, the words of Hebrews 13:5 and Joshua 1:5 are the words of Jesus Christ. Second, these words are applied to the Lord as the one who has established the monastic way of life. He is the beginning and the end of the monastic life as well as the one who travels with monks, constantly assuring them with these words from Hebrews and Joshua. Sarapion interprets this verse as words from Jesus Christ, the creator of the monastic way

---

189 Again, I refer the reader to my essay "A 'Doctrine of Scripture' from the Eastern Orthodox Tradition: A Reflection on the Desert Father Saint Sarapion of Thmuis," (op. cit.).
190 PG 40,928B. Heb 13:5 and Josh 1:5.

of life, to those who travel this course of life.

Later in the letter, Sarapion mentions Abraham as an exemplar, only this time for a different reason—the monastic calling.

> Long ago, God said to Abraham, 'Leave your land and your family and [go] here to the land I will show you.' And when he heard, Abraham went forth. I see you also grasping the Word of God so that you might follow Abraham and enjoy his blessing.[191]

The phrase "Word of God" is important. The phrase suggests not only that Abraham leaves everything to follow God's command, but that in doing so, he follows the Word of God (the Son of God). This is suggested by the larger Egyptian monastic context. Samuel Rubenson provides a critical translation of the letters of Anthony (of whom Sarapion was a disciple) in which the Syriac version of the first letter links the ascetic life to the call of Abraham, which comes from the Word of God.[192] This same connection between the Word of God and Abraham's call and the monastic life is found in St. John Cassian's *Conferences* 3.3–4, which he attributes to Abba Paphnutios.[193] Given this context, it seems very likely that Sarapion presents this passage consistently with how he presents Hebrews 13:5/Joshua 1:5, where the words in the text attributed to God are words of the Word, Jesus the Christ.

Following this reference to the call of Abraham, Sarapion proceeds immediately to a quote from Lamentations. "'It is good for a man, whenever he takes up a yoke from his youth. He will sit alone and be silent.' Your withdrawal explains this."[194] For Sarapion, this verse applies in a literal fashion to the monastic life. The phrase "your withdrawal explains this" displays the hermeneutical assumption behind his use of this verse from Lamentations. For Sarapion, the living of the monastic life opens one to the meaning of this verse. Interpretation is not primarily an intellectual activity, but a *tropos*, a manner of living.

Even the words of Christ apply to the monks and the monastic life,

---

191 PG 40,929 D. Gen 12:1.
192 S. Rubenson, *The Letters of St. Anthony: Monasticism and the Making of a Saint* (Minneapolis 1995) 197.
193 John Cassian, *Conferences*, trans. C. Luibheid (New York 1985).
194 PG 40,929D. Lam 3:27–28.

something evidenced when Sarapion quotes from the words of Christ, applying them to the monks:

> A common man does not deceive a soldier, but neither do the demons, who have fled your piety. For God, who gives gifts to you, said, 'Behold, I have given you authority to tread upon serpents and scorpions and upon all the power of the enemy and nothing will injure you.'[195]

Serpents and scorpions being allegorically understood, the words of Jesus refer to the demon-conquering powers of the monks. As above in other examples, the words Christ speaks are words spoken to and about the monks.

One should also recall a use of the Psalms noted above when discussing the Stoic context to the letter. Sarapion writes:

> [B]ecause you clearly acknowledge your dignity and glory, you have prevailed in perfecting your reward by being increasingly vigilant because of the hope of things to come and by singing David's phrase, "Take courage! Let your heart be strengthened and wait on the Lord".[196]

Through the monks' vigilance, the words of David from Psalm 26 have become their words so that they sing the Psalms along with David. One senses the spacio-temporal distance between the monks and the biblical figures collapsing. The words of the Bible are words of the Word, Jesus the Christ, and the monastic life, because it interprets these words, collapses the distance between the biblical figures and the monks themselves.

In one section in particular, Sarapion lists a series of biblical referents, ending with the words of Christ from Matthew 5.8.

> A paradise of delights will be established for you. And the doors of paradise, which Adam's transgression closed, your desire for God will open. For heaven was established on your behalf, so that you might meet face to face with the apostles, see the prophets, behold the martyrs, embrace all

---

195 937A. Luke 10:19.
196 PG 40,941A. Ps 26:14 (27:14).

the righteous, spend time with the angels. There you will be blessed and will be more blessed in your life thereafter. There you will see John the Baptiser, the originator of your asceticism, who was nourished in the desert and prominent in his asceticism. There you will see the most courageous Job (a participant in your sufferings and an admirer of your endurance) surrounded with many glories. There you will see your forefather Abraham, who has become a genuine admirer of your hospitality. There the most mild and ascetic David (whose life daily encourages you) will meet you. And, lest the naming of each of the righteous might prolong this letter, you will see Christ himself as the head of all his good people saying, 'Blessed are the pure in heart, for they shall see God'.[197]

In this case, the fall of Adam (the cause of which he does not specify but earlier linked to gluttony[198]) closed heaven but the monks' desire for God opens heaven again. Clearly, the monastic life reverses the effects of the fall. The reference to the gates of heaven calls to mind biblical exemplars who become types for the monks as well as presently living examples in heaven to imitate and even admirers of the monks themselves. Finally, Sarapion gives the words of Christ an anagogical twist by stating that the words from his beatitudes (concerning the pure in heart) will be proclaimed about all his followers in heaven, which includes the faithful monks.[199]

---

197 PG 40,937C. Matt 5:8.
198 See PG 40,936D, where he writes: "For you also have acquired the taste for cheap foods, you are satisfied with drinking water, in order not to exaggerate the roles [of food and drink] for the benefit of the stomach and most of all because the deviation ($παράβασις$) came into being by Adam's tasting". See Gen 3:1–24, especially 3:8.
199 It is worth noting that D. Burton-Christie also cites the attachment of certain virtues with particular biblical figures in the *Sayings of the Desert Fathers*. See *The Word in the Desert: Scripture and the Quest for Holiness in Early Christian Monasticism* (Oxford 1993). For example, he quotes Abba John the Persian as saying: "I have been hospitable like Abraham, meek like Moses, holy like Aaron, patient like Job, humble like David, a hermit like John, filled with compunction like Jeremiah, a master like Paul, full of faith like Peter, wise like Solomon" (168). See John the Persian 4, PG 65,237D–240A. He also cites Abba Nisterus and the *Lausiac History* for similar examples (168). See Nisterus 2, PG 65,305D–308A and *Lausiac History* 14.4. Sarapion may be providing an anagogical twist, but he draws upon the tradition of the Desert Fathers.

To summarise: in his *Letter to the Monks* Sarapion presents the reader with a unique hermeneutic, although one also fully consistent with the approach displayed in *Against the Manichaeans*. There are five discernable components to this hermeneutic. First, Sarapion believes that the overarching subject of the Bible is the incarnate Word, Jesus the Christ. This can be deduced from his belief that citations from either the Old or New Testaments may be read as words of the Word. Second, the incarnate Word himself establishes the monastic life and its conclusion (the Heavenly Kingdom) while also being a "fellow-traveller" along the way. It is because Jesus the Christ has created monasticism that the biblical verses may apply to the monks. Third, this monastic life, established and sustained by Christ, opens the Bible to its meaning. In so doing, the spacio-temporal distance between the monks and the Fathers in the Bible collapses. The monks are spiritual contemporaries of the figures of the biblical text, capable of even surpassing those figures and being admired by them. Fourth, the meaning is derived through a pesher-like approach, where all aspects of the biblical text refer to this Christocentric monasticism. Whether Sarapion uses literal readings or more allegorical readings, they all are revealed by this Christocentric monasticism and speak of it as well.

The fourth point makes it clear that a circular activity occurs— that which unlocks the Scriptures is what is spoken by the Scriptures. The first, second and third points serve to remind us that Sarapion's hermeneutic is not a hermeneutic of monasticism *in se*, but a Christocentric hermeneutic, where monasticism is understood as being caught up in the life of Christ so that the monks strive after him, glorify him, and reveal him. This leads us to a fifth and final point. Sarapion's hermeneutic is a *lived* hermeneutic, it is a *tropos*, a manner of living.[200] Sarapion concerns himself not with presenting a textual key to unlock the Scriptures, but a spiritual life caught up in the life of Christ. Just as the Word Incarnate presents himself through the words of the text, so, too, the words of the Word become the words of those who

---

200   Burton-Christie likewise notes the importance of monasticism as a lived hermeneutic for the desert fathers. See *The Word in the Desert*, 300, where he writes: "The ultimate expression of the desert hermeneutic was a *person*, one who embodied the sacred texts and who drew others out of themselves into a world of infinite possibilities".

faithfully live the Christian monastic life. Sarapion understands monasticism to be a Christocentric interpretation of the Bible.

In keeping with an encomium to *proficientes*-monks, Sarapion's hermeneutic in *Letter to the Monks* displays a different flare than what may be found in *Against the Manichaeans*. In this letter, he portrays monasticism itself as a lived Christocentric interpretation. The monastic life interprets the text. In so doing, the spacio-temporal distance between the monks and the biblical exemplars collapses and the biblical exemplars actually admire the life of the monks (who have progressed so far in living the life of Christ).

However, such an approach also displays continuity. Just as the economies of Christ are the "hypothesis" of the Scriptures in the treatise, so in the *Letter to the Monks*, the life of Christ opens unlocks the meaning of Bible. The monks certainly live out the interpretation, but the interpretation they live is a Christocentric one, one centred on the life of Christ, such that the Bible becomes the words of the Word and the interpretation of those words is the monastic life, which lives the interpretation given by the Word himself. This approach is not the same as what one finds in *Against the Manichaeans*, but it in no way contradicts that approach and, if anything, would seem to exhibit a fulfilment of that approach because the monks, being Christian *proficientes*, live out that interpretation that links the Law, Psalms, and Prophets to the Gospels through the economies of Christ.

Sarapion of Thmuis as the Author of the Letter to the Monks

Contrary to previous scholarship, especially Casey, Fitschen categorises the letter as being among the pseudepigraphic writings. Fitschen argues that a comparison of Codex Vaticanus Graecus and Codex Mosquensis S. Synod. proves that Sarapion could not have been the author. A phrase in the former that refers to the *Life of Anthony*, reads as οὗ καὶ ὁ βίος ἔγγραπτος παρ' ὑμῖν διασώζεται ("whose written *Life* is also preserved among you").²⁰¹ The Moscow manuscript refers to Anthony as ὁ περιώνυμος ("he who is widely-famous"), a term not in the Vaticanus manuscript, and then goes on to render the passage just given as, οὗ καὶ ὁ βίος ἔγγραπτος παρ' ὑμῖν μέχρι καὶ νῦν σώζεται ("whose written *Life* is being kept even up to now among you").²⁰² Fitschen believes that it is significant that the words μέχρι καὶ νῦν are included in the Moscow manuscript. These words imply, he believes, a situation wherein the *Life of Anthony* is not a relatively new publication, but rather one that has been around for some time and is being preserved, thus suggesting that someone wrote this letter after the lifetime of Sarapion.

Fitschen provides other reasons he does not assign authorship to Sarapion of Thmuis, based upon the phrase, ὑμεῖς γὰρ αὐτοῖς καὶ συνδιατρίψατε καὶ οἱ πατέρες ὑμῶν ("For you have spent time with them and so have your fathers").²⁰³ Fitschen argues that since there is no reason to suppose that Anthony was alive, there's really no reason to suppose that any of the fathers (Anthony, Amoun, John, or Macarius) were alive when the letter was written.²⁰⁴ He notes that Amoun died before Anthony and that John could be either John of Lycopolis or John the "the maimed" (κολοβός) and Macarius is most likely Macarius the Egyptian. The last two names would seem to be the most problematic for one arguing on behalf of Sarapion as the author, since, as Fitschen observes, John of Lycopolis, the earlier of the two Johns, died in 394 and Macarius the Egyptian died in 390. Fitschen states that the latest evidence for Sarapion still being alive is around 370, in his correspondence with the future heresiarch Apollinaris. From this, he suggests that even if we ascribe a long life (like Anthony's) that would go beyond 370, we are still left wondering why the author of the letter did not report something from their lives. Granted, "them," in the passage just cited, could refer to the kings (or even the recipients of the miracles performed

---

201 PG 40,940B. This passage is also given in Fitschen, 80. The larger context of 940B-C reads: "From you has come forth Father Anthony, on account of the highest life, whose written *Life* is also preserved among you. So, too, also, Father Amoun, Father John, and Father Macarius, who have valiantly shone forth in pre-eminence [...] Hearing these things, kings marvelled, enthusiastically praising God. You know these things more accurately than we do. For you have spent time with them and so have your fathers".
202 Fitschen, *Serapion*, 81.
203 PG 40,940B. Fitschen, *Serapion*, 80–81.
204 Fitschen, *Serapion*, 81.

by Amoun, John, and/or Macarius) but this would not undercut Fitschen's point, which is that the sentence in question suggests that the monks were contemporaries with Amoun, John, and Macarius.

Additionally, the tone of the entire work strikes Fitschen as an extended encomium, where the highly exalted monks are not chided until the end, and then only by way of encouraging them not to end the race they have begun.[205] Therefore, Fitschen dates the letter to the 5th century and assigns its author the designation of "pseudo-Serapion".

McNary-Zak addresses Fitschen's contention that Sarapion did not author the letter.[206] With respect to the importance Fitschen places on the words μέχρι καὶ νῦν that are included in the Moscow manuscript, McNary-Zak retorts that Fitschen's arguments "are significant, yet inconclusive".[207] Her reasoning is that although the Moscow manuscript (a partial manuscript that includes much of this letter) is a century older than the Vatican manuscript (with the complete text), there is no reason for privileging the former.[208] She also cites the parallels mentioned by Casey and Outtier.[209] Unfortunately, McNary-Zak limits her response to Fitschen to these comments in her endnotes.

In addition to her own rebuttal of Fitschen's argument on the basis of a manuscript variant, McNary-Zak's reminder of the vocabulary similarities that Casey notes[210] as well as a few similarities between the *Letter to the Monks* and the *Letter on the Death of Anthony*, which Outtier highlights,[211] points us in another important direction. Although she does not reproduce their arguments in her footnote rebuttal to Fitschen, both deserve to be presented in light of their significance.

Casey observes that the following characteristic words by Sarapion, as attested by *Against the Manichaeans*, are found in the *Letter to the Monks*: πρᾶγμα, διάνοια, σωτήρ, προαίρεσις, βοάω, and μάταιον.[212] Πρᾶγμα is found in *Against the Manichaeans* 4.5; 9.14; 15.11,19;

205 Ibid., 82.
206 Ibid., 80–2.
207 McNary-Zak, *Letters*, 13, n. 46.
208 Ibid., 14, n. 46.
209 Ibid., 13, n. 45.
210 Casey, *Manichaeans*, 13, n. 3.
211 Outtier, *Lettres des pères du désert*, 151.
212 Casey, *Manichaeans*, 13, n. 3.

18.13,17; 23.13; 30.34; 38.14; 40.19,73; 41.12; 42.1; 46.44; 47.14; 49.43; 50.1,44; 53.20,22.[213] It is found in the *Letter to the Monks* in PG 40,928 and 933. Διάνοια is found in *Against the Manichaeans* 1.3,7,12; 6.4; 9.4; 10.19; 16.3; 19.22; 20.7; 27.24; 28.2; 41.24; 42.15; 44.20,33,37; 45.15,20,25,27; 46. 21,24,28; 48.12; 49.26; 51.11; 52.34; 53.50,59,70; 54.6.[214] It is found in the *Letter to the Monks* in PG 40,928 and 935. While Casey does not include σωτήρ in his list of distinctive vocabulary from *Against the Manichaeans*, he is correct to note it as a word in that treatise as well as in the *Letter to the Monks*. The term can be found throughout the treatise, occurring, for example, in 53.9, 25 and Casey notes three occurrences of the term in the letter (in PG 40,928).[215] Προαίρεσις exists in *Against the Manichaeans* 4.6,10,14; 8.17; 15.8; 23.28,29; 24.5–6; 25.5; 29.11,29; 30.40,45; 41.7.[216] It is likewise found in the letter in PG 40,928. Βοάω is written in *Against the Manichaeans* 1.7; 10.15,16; 9.8; 20.16; 37.25; 39.30; 40.25,67; 44.10; 46.5; 48.10; 49.15; 50.21,27,32; 53.19,25.[217] It occurs primarily as a means of introducing biblical quotations, a usage consistent with its occurrence in the letter in PG 40,928 as a means of introducing Philippians 3:8. Μάταιον is the weakest connection, as it is found only three times in *Against the Manichaeans* 53.63 as a quotation from Ecclesiastes 1:2. However, of its occurrences in PG 40,932, 933, and 936, the first precedes a quotation from Ecclesiastes 5:11, a passage near the one quoted in *Against the Manichaeans*.

Outtier, as already stated, noted similarities between the *Letter to the Monks* and the *Letter on the Death of Anthony*. Specifically, he notes two phrases found in both the *Letter to the Monks* and the Armenian version of the *Letter on the Death of Anthony*, which he says argues in favour of the Armenian version.[218] He suggests that the reference to the monks as great intercessors parallels PG 40,929B, which speaks of Alexandria as being blessed for having the monks as intercessors and notes the phrase "holy hands", which is found in PG 40,936C. He also

---

213   Ibid., 11.
214   Ibid., 8.
215   Ibid., 13, n. 3.
216   Ibid., 8.
217   Ibid., 11.
218   Outtier, *Lettres des pères du désert*, 151.

cites the observation of Draguet, based in part upon Casey, that the style of the *Letter to the Monks* is similar to that of the *Letter on the Death of Anthony*, both letters having balanced sentences with an inclination toward antithesis.[219]

Indeed, antithesis can be found throughout the *Letter to the Monks*. For example, Sarapion writes, "You are not a thicket of trees, so that wild animals might dwell in you, the blood-thirsty herd of the adversarial powers. But you are the garden that has enclosed the keeping of the law and steadfastness with the honourable stones".[220] One may also consider another passage (cited earlier):

> A common man does not deceive a soldier, but neither do the demons, who have fled your piety. [...] You have not been enrolled in the army of a human king in order that you might see the slaughter of fellow men in war, but you have been enrolled in the army of Christ in order that you might see the defeat of demons. [...] Furthermore, you have not been enrolled in the army in order that you might pour out human blood, but you have been enrolled in the army of God in order that you might continuously pour out your prayer to his face.[221]

These examples demonstrate that Sarapion uses well-balanced antithesis in the *Letter to the Monks*.

The previously cited opening passage from the *Letter to Bishop Eudoxius*, (which is almost entirely a piece of balanced, antithetical statements), shows that antithesis is characteristic of Sarapion's style: "Do not lose heart in suffering, but take heart in believing. And do not fall down when sick, but maintain your powers by not sinning. Do not consider sickness grievous. Sin alone is grievous."[222]

In addition to the argument by McNary-Zak against Fitschen's emphasis on the manuscript variant and her indication of the similarities elicited by Casey and Outtier, a few more arguments may be made. First, Fitschen's assumption that all the desert fathers named in the let-

---

219 Ibid., 120. See Draguet, "Une letter de Sérapion", 22.
220 PG 40,933D.
221 PG 40,937A.
222 PG 40,924C.

ter must be dead is unwarranted (or at the very least unnecessary). Second, the hermeneutical and philosophical (Stoic) continuity between the writings discussed here provide a compelling piece of evidence in Sarapion's favour. Third, writing to the monks as though they are Christian, Stoic *proficientes* addresses Fitschen's concern regarding the fact that the letter reads as an encomium, as does attributing traditional, Egyptian religious roles to the monks.

The assumption that Amoun, John, and Macarius must all be dead strikes me as an incredible assumption, as the desert monastic literature attests to desert fathers attaining fame well before their deaths. To cite but two examples, one could highlight the cases of Anthony the Great and Abba Poemen. Someone, possibly Sarapion, or several people including Sarapion, penned the *Life of Anthony* by 355, just prior to Anthony's death, suggesting that a significant following developed during his own lifetime.[223] With regard to Poemen, a story from the *Sayings of the Desert Fathers* claims that his arrival in Egypt resulted in a famous (but here anonymous) old monk losing his followers to Poemen.[224] As noted above, even Sarapion himself attests to the known reputation of the monks to whom he was writing.

With respect to the Stoicised expression of Christianity within these pieces, there exists complete conformity. The *Letter to the Monks* presents the monks as Christianised, Stoic *proficientes* who, having transcended the *adiaphora* of the worldly life, have need only to continue to endure monastic hardships in order to be shown worthy of an existence with the sage they follow—Jesus the Christ. Sarapion evokes both Stoic themes and vocabulary in writing this letter. Likewise, in the *Letter to Bishop Eudoxius*, Sarapion provides Christianised, Stoic advice to a sick and suffering bishop. Bishop Eudoxius is to concern himself with avoiding sin and acquiring virtue in the midst of his affliction. *Against the Manichaeans* also bases itself upon a line of Christianised Stoic thought.

Both the concept of monks as *proficientes* and the indigenous,

---

223 McNary-Zak, Letters, 88. Additionally, the *Life of Anthony* has a very early and widely-distributed attestation. See Jerome's Illustrious Men 87, 88, 125, Gregory Nazianzus' Orations 21.5, and, more importantly, the First Greek Life of Pachomius 99.
224 *The Sayings of the Desert Fathers, the Alphabetical Collection*, trans. Benedicta Ward (Kalamazoo 1975) Pi 4.

Egyptian religious themes produce a rebuttal to Fitschen's claim that Sarapion would not have written an encomium for the monks but that it would have come from a later author idealizing those monks. Since he views the monks as *proficientes*, at least in this case, Sarapion does not lecture the monks or seek to exert his episcopal powers. Perhaps he does in other letters. Future manuscript finds might inform us, but with respect to this letter, one written to a group he considers *proficientes*, an encomium seems highly appropriate. Furthermore, because Sarapion utilises the indigenous Egyptian religious desire for intercessors on behalf of cosmic order, the monks take on a role formerly attributed to the Pharaohs and later, by the author of the *Apocalypse of Elijah*, at least, the Christian martyrs (especially with respect to their bodily presence in the cosmos). By transcending the *adiaphora* of the world, and enduring monastic hardships, the monks become *proficientes* who sustain cosmic order through their intercessory powers. An encomium hardly seems inappropriate in such a situation.[225]

Accounting for the various facets of how Sarapion reflects upon suffering and hardship, especially within the monastic life, provides us with evidence in favour of Sarapion's authorship of the *Letter to the Monks* both with respect to the continuity with Sarapion's unquestioned writings (specifically, the *Letter to Bishop Eudoxius*) and with respect to reasons for the letter's format as an encomium. Sarapion also exhibits hermeneutical consistency with his *Against the Manichaeans*.

---

225 Not even Sarapion's milieu would preclude such a style of letter. S.K. Stowers, *Letter Writing in Greco-Roman Antiquity* (Philadelphia 1986), 84–85, has already noted at least one prominent example of a letter of praise, which comes from a fourth-century-Egyptian-Christian context. This letter is taken from H.I. Bell (ed.), *Jews and Christians in Egypt; the Jewish troubles in Alexandria and the Athanasian Controversy*, with three Coptic texts, edited by W. E. Crum (Westport, CT 1972). With respect to the Egyptian milieu, M.L. Colish's assessment of John Cassian's significance for Stoicism and monasticism should be revised. Colish believes that Cassian's Christianised, monastic Stoicism proves to be a rather independent venture. See M.L. Colish, *The Stoic Tradition from Aniquity to the Early Middle Ages*, Vol. 2, *Stoicism in Christian Latin Thought through the Sixth Century* (Leiden 1985) 115 and 120. Sarapion's Stoicised Christian monasticism calls into question Colish's claims to Cassian's independence inasmuch as Sarapion may well be witnessing to what already was a reality in Egypt. Even in the case that Sarapion helped formulate and develop such an approach, one would have to wonder how independent Cassian could have been since Sarapion was formulating this Stoicised Christian monasticism prior to Cassian's interactions with the desert fathers of Egypt. A comparison of Sarapion and Cassian on this score could prove helpful.

When added to the vocabulary similarities noted by Casey and the other similarities mentioned by Outtier (and Draguet), especially in regard to antithesis, as well as the suggestion that Fitschen's assumption (that the desert fathers named in the letter are dead) is unnecessary, and that there is no compelling reason to accept the priority of the Moscow manuscript, the case in favour of Sarapion's authorship looks quite compelling. Unless and until highly provocative evidence necessitates attributing the *Letter to the Monks* to a "pseudo-Sarapion", we would do well to accept Sarapion's authorship of the *Letter to the Monks*.

TEXT IN TRANSLATION

St. Sarapion, Bishop of Thmuis: A Letter to Bishop Eudoxius

Do not lose heart in suffering, but take heart in believing. And do not fall down when sick, but maintain your powers by not sinning. Do not consider sickness grievous. Sin alone is grievous.

For being ill is common to both good and evil men. But we see that sinning is something peculiar to base men. And the one who is ill has a sickness that ends with his death. But the one who has sinned will find that even after his funeral, the sin is still there. Illness lasts until the funeral, [925] but it is unable after the funeral to afflict the one who had died. Sin lurks and hides in the living, but clings even more to those who have died, and shows its fiery nature[1] and avenges itself on the one who has sinned.

I have written these things to you, my most longed-for brother lest you altogether lose heart while keeping yourself in Christ. It is necessary to bear the confusions of life and fitting to endure its tumults and look to the goal and know that God presides. When he acts providentially, he still leads the way and, when he seems absent, he approaches again.[2] The church is never forsaken. For the gates of Hades will not prevail against her.[3] Therefore, display the state of your virtue to the all-seeing God, in order that you might be of good repute in all things.

1　Literally, "flame" (φλόγα).
2　Literally, "And when he goes back a little, he again leads the way. And when he gives way a little, he again approaches" (καὶ ὀλίγον ἐπάνεις πάλιν ἡγεμονεύει καὶ ὀλίγον συγχῶρων πάλιν προΐσταται).
3　Matt 16:18.

We would not have taken the pains to call you lest we should seem to leave the city [without contacting you].[4]

---

4   This final sentence is quite ambiguous. R.P. Casey, *Manichaeans*, 72, understands this sentence to be a response to Eudoxios' desire to be invited to call upon Sarapion. Holding a similar position, Fitschen suggests replacing ἐπασχόμεθα with ἐπεσχόμεθα, so that rather than saying something like "we would not have taken the pains to call you," the phrase should read "we would not be able to induce you to call." Fitschen, *Serapion*, 64–66, translates the sentence, "we, however, might not be able to induce you to call, therewith we bind you not to depart from the city." The question becomes whether σε is the subject or object of καλέσαι. Being in the accusative, it could be the subject, as Fitschen has it, which causes Fitschen to make his suggested change with respect to the verb ἐπασχόμεθα. If, however, σε is the object, then the sentence could retain the verb as it is and read something like, "We would not have taken the pains to call you lest we should seem to leave the city [without contacting you]." The difficulty here, of course, is that it would seem more natural to place δόξωμεν ("seem") in passive voice rather than active, as it is in the Greek. I leave it to the reader to be the final judge of the sentence: ἡμεῖς δὲ καλέσαι σε οὐκ ἂν ἐπασχόμεθα ἵνα μὴ δόξωμεν τῆς πόλεως ἀφιστᾶν.

An Epistle of the Most Blessed and Hallowed Bishop Sarapion to the Monks*

Most Beloved,

I praise your devotion and bless your life, you blessed monks of God, because [928] while having a nature common to everyone, you do not have the same purpose. For having contemplated what is great, you furnished your mind with these heavenly matters alone, so that after having inquired closely into the help of the divine teachings from heaven, you might be found [to have] the same conduct as the blessed angels, whose glory awaits you and whose blessedness awaits you. For being men who have advanced beyond men,[1] you were not seduced by human reasoning nor have the things of life that seem desirable been able to lessen the intensity of your desire for God. But in general, having been set apart in all things, you have one aim — to please God. And your struggle for a good reputation has been discussed by everyone. Neither an abundance of wealth nor the promises of gifts set before you has acquired this good zeal for you, but righteous faith and loving thought, with God the Saviour acting as your mediator and being well pleased. The Leader who is both the originator and the accomplisher of this acceptable and good way of life is Jesus the Christ. He is also the one who gives to you monks a power to endure and a most worthy end, and who secures, for all those desiring to be saved, an assured course, one which you have been eager to travel from the beginning. You have, as a fellow-traveller, the Saviour Lord who says: "I do not neglect you nor abandon you".[2]

Because of this, not one impediment has been able to hinder your heavenly purpose — not a desire for wealth, not a memory of parents, nor family inheritances, nor conversations with brothers, not a family will, not luxuries such as baths and drinking bouts, not the intervention of friends,[3] not the glories of the world, but having despised everything, you cry out against these works, declaring with the Apostle's saying: "I regard all things as refuse in order that I might gain Christ".[4] This is why you live in the desert with fasts, purifications, and ascetical acts, appeasing God with pure prayers.

And not one earthly ruler is ever fearful to you, not a magistrate, nor a judge, nor a governor, nor any other authority. "For the law is not laid down for the righteous but the lawless and disobedient, the godless and sinful, those

---

*Translated from PG 40, 925-941.
[1] Alternatively, and more literally, this phrase could read "and having come from men" (καὶ ἐξ ἀνθρώπων προελθόντες).
[2] Heb 13:5. See also Josh 1:5.
[3] Alternatively "not incidents with friends" (οὐ φίλων συντυχίαι).
[4] Phil 3:8.

who kill their fathers and mothers, murderers, fornicators and homosexuals[5], perjurers, and whatever else is contrary to correct teaching."[6] "For rulers are not a terror to good deeds, but to bad." And again: "Do you wish not to fear authority? Do good and you will have its praise".[7] Therefore, praises are justly [given] to you, just as is the harsh punishment to those warned against opposing rulers.[8]

God singled you out for himself to be a special people, "zealous for good works".[9] "You are the light of the world",[10] the Saviour has said, of whom the zeal is the same, the work is the same, the approval is the same, and the reward is the same. Therefore, you are blessed—even thrice-blessed, [oh] most honourable monks for God. Who among you is worthy of commending your life? For you, daily and nightly activities are psalms, hymns, spiritual songs, and works fitting for God. For love governs you, [929] treasure of the angels. The peace that encompasses the heavens has been established among you. Your way of life is not to love money. You are always content with necessity, being vigorous in fasting, more vigorous in prayer. Vigils are completed in wakefulness by you every day. "Shine your light",[11] said the Lord, and that which he has said is coming to light. You have not cared about worldly love nor the things in this world. Therefore you are blessed before God and the world is also blessed through you. The deserts are being exalted through you and the inhabited world is being saved by your prayers. The rain is sent down upon the earth by your supplications, the earth produces green plants, and the trees, laden with fruits, yield undamaged fruit. The river, flooding yearly and watering the whole of Egypt, forming into marshy lakes and distributing a great amount into the seas, makes known the power of your supplications. For if (as it is written)[12] Elijah, who was a passionate man like all others, both held back the rain and restored it again by prayer, and the heavens sent rains and the earth grew her fruit, how much more effective will your intercessions be for gaining advantages for us by your prayers?

Therefore the city of Alexandria is blessed by having you as mediators. The

---

[5] Literally "male-bedders", or men who lie with other men as with women.
[6] 1 Tim 1:9-10.
[7] Rom 13:3.
[8] That Sarapion maintains obedience and good works with regard to civil authorities should be noted as evidence of the extent to which he held to this principle, given the tumultuous times in which he lived. In terms of good deeds and righteous conduct, it is possible that this sentence also has a double meaning, as Sarapion speaks of hell as a finite reality that serves the purpose of providing corrective punishments for the eventual salvation of all (see *Against the Manichaeans* 29 and 30).
[9] Titus 2:14.
[10] Matt 5:14.
[11] Sarapion paraphrases from Matt 5:16, which turns the phrase into a command.
[12] Jas 5:17-18 and 3 Kgs 17-18, especially 17:1 and 18: 40-6.

cities of the Sodomites would not have been reduced to ashes if ten righteous people were living there.[13] Nor again would other cities have been overturned if they had shared in your holiness. The friends of the God-fearing Job, who were hard to deal with, were saved from death because of him, as it is written: "My servant Job will pray for you because I will only put up with him. For if it had not been for him, I would have destroyed all of you".[14] Formerly, the Jewish people sinned when the servant of God received the law. By neglecting propriety, the people (always without understanding and foolish) annoyed Aaron, saying: "Make gods for us, ones who will go before us".[15] When they transgressed, the Lord became angry with them and said: "Moses, Moses, descend quickly for the people have acted lawlessly".[16] But having gone down and seen the transgression, he answered God, saying: "If you can forgive their sin, forgive, but if not then also erase me from the book which you have written".[17] Oh, how great is the representation through the saints! Oh, how much will your prayers bring forth advantages for our prayers, to induce the goodwill of God! Oh, how great is the repose that will be laid up for you, who are eager to be united to God! Oh, with how many goods will you be fulfilled, you who have left behind father, mother, and brothers.

Long ago God said to Abraham: "Leave your land and your family and [go] here to the land that I will show you".[18] And when he heard, Abraham went forth. I see you also grasping the Word of God so that you might follow Abraham and enjoy his blessing.[19]

"It is good for a man, whenever he takes up a yoke from his youth. He will sit alone and be silent".[20] Your [932]withdrawal explains this. Wealth did not entice you nor did the beauty of women mislead you, but as if you were incorporeal beings, you trampled upon opposing pleasures by your reverence for the divine. You were not riveted to the cares of the world but you shunned

---

[13] Gen 18:32.
[14] Job 42:8.
[15] Exod 32:1.
[16] Exod 32:7.
[17] Exod 32:32.
[18] Gen 12:1.
[19] I have chosen to capitalise "Word" because connections between the Word of God, Abraham's call, and the monastic life are present in the monastic, Egyptian milieu. Rubenson, *The Letters of St Anthony*, provides a critical translation of the letters of Anthony in which the Syriac version of the first letter links the ascetic life to the call of Abraham and this call comes from the Word of God. The validity of my interpretation would seem to be strengthened, given Sarapion's close connection with Anthony, though I do not intend to make too much of a sixth-century Syriac text. This same connection between the Word of God and Abraham's call and the monastic life is found in John Cassian's *Conferences* 3.3-4, which he attributes to Abba Paphnutius.
[20] Lam 3:27-28.

their vanity. Simple bread and salt and drinkable water are more pleasurable for you in the desert than the city delicacies and wicked enjoyments. For an old proverb says, "a crumb enjoyed in peace is better than a house with many goods and ill-gotten offerings with strife".[21]

You are free in all things, oh monks, most divinely favoured by God! A wife does not trouble you concerning womanly adornments. Sons or daughters are not harassing you by bringing disagreeable requests to you. Nor does a servant, after stealing valuables, run away. Nor does a concern about wealth steal your sleep. For "to the one who has been satisfied with wealth", Ecclesiastes declares, "there is not one who permits him to sleep".[22]

These are the sweet things of life and those that are most desired in life. Whenever someone marries in a city, it is a source of crises, a necessity of expenditures. Is one's wife pregnant? Has she given birth? Has the baby been born? The man's concern will be how he will fulfil all the thoughts of his wife. Is the child born a girl? The man is disgusted that he is being robbed concerning the dowry. Was the child born a boy? His countenance is joyful for a short time. Not long after, the child has collapsed from sickness. Being a calamity for the man, he does not cease calling physicians. He will give many things if the child will be saved. Going to his friends with his eyes cast down, he meets them saying: "Pray! Because my child is sick. If he should die, I will hang myself!" The friends console him. But God provides life for the family's goodwill. The little child gets better, grows, gets taller, and becomes a youth. Various teachers take over this one and, as he grows, he is instructed according to the world. He becomes then a young man, suitable for marital union. His father is occupied with marriage. Everything was prepared; the bride-chamber was prepared, but death suddenly snatched away the young man. The unforeseen calamity is unbearable to the father. The young man is buried. Henceforth, there are moanings and lamentations when the father[23] arrives at the funeral shouting loud lamentations and hitting his head with his hands, shaking and striking his face, while continuously saying: "Woe is me! Woe is me!" And being very distressed by the calamity, he often falls into serious illness, and being consumed little by little, he henceforth cries out for death.

Learn, most honoured monks of God, of how many cares Christ has freed you. Learn of how many calamities you have avoided. Know what sort of life you are pursuing. You are like angels in your daily life. For just as in the resurrection from the dead, when people "neither marry nor are given in marriage, but the righteous are like angels in heaven",[24] so, living together

---

[21] Prov 17:1. Migne cites 15:17, but Zirnheld correctly cites 17:1. See B. Outtier, *Lettres des pères du désert,* 136.
[22] Eccl 5:11.
[23] Literally, "the one arriving" or "the one who arrives".
[24] Matt 22:30. The PG mistakenly refers to Matt 22:20.

in the same manner, you also have anticipated the future existence by your desire. Therefore, who would not bless you, who have chosen a life free from distractions? Who would not proclaim your way of life in the desert? Who would not desire your peaceful solitude?

Councils [933] and juridical inquiries concerning civil matters are organised in cities. Who will satisfy the bellies of the dancers and actors and musicians? Who will waste his wealth with lawless and profane theatre games? And yet, you are free from seeking these things on account of the Lord. You are not subject to state or civil services, nor does the hand of some tax-collector knock on your door in order that you might pay the tax. No one in the imperial guard does violence against you. Things such as these do happen, but you will not dwell in prison after being falsely accused. Nor shall your feet receive shackles, being falsely accused of great crimes in order that you might pay taxes. Nor will your hands be bound with small cords on account of some other circumstance. You know neither the extortions of soldiers nor the inhuman ridicule of the militia. You do not pursue commerce in order that you might collect wealth by means of false oaths, knowing that "what little belongs to a righteous person is better than the great wealth of sinners".[25] A creditor does not awaken you as you sleep by bringing the contract, nor has he presented charges to the magistrate in accordance with your written agreements. Nor do you bemoan the magnitude of the interest being demanded. But neither have you feared the sea that, when suddenly aroused by a storm, it might utterly destroy your ship's cargo and you, a rich man, might immediately be found to be a poor man.

These things are the pursuits of life. These are the affairs of life. Those bound in marriage endure these things. But you dwell in the desert free from distractions, concerned with a single shining life. Oh, how pre-eminent an honour your holy and divine character has! Oh, how much spiritual sweetness does it exude! Oh how great a vow have you made! No word is capable of praising this! Oh, the binding promise of heaven! Oh, the vow that unites one to God! Oh, the vow that makes one like the angels! Oh, the vow that preserves what is in the image of God! Oh, the vow that has placed one beside God! Oh, the vow that is most valued by God! Oh, the vow by which the cosmos is saved! Whoever blesses you would rightly say, "Blessed are the ones blameless in the way, the ones who walk in the law of the Lord".[26] For those attending to this law day and night are "as the tree planted by the brooks of waters, which shall give its fruit in season and its foliage will not fall off and whatever he does will prosper".[27]

---

[25] Ps 36:16 (37:16).
[26] Ps 118:1 (119:1).
[27] Ps 1:2-3.

So, therefore, being the ones bearing fruit by word and deed, you are able to say, more confidently, to God: "Let my kinsman come down into his garden and eat the fruit of his fruit-trees".[28] For each one of you, oh monks rightly beloved by God, is a garden of Christ containing all kinds of trees cultivated by the commandments and the keeping of the law. You are not a thicket of trees, so that wild[29] animals might dwell in you, the bloodthirsty herd of the adversarial powers. But you are the garden that has enclosed the keeping of the law and steadfastness with the honourable stones. Therefore, you were not captives of the devil, but were ensnared by the drag-net of Christ from the bitter confusion of the world.

A married person is divided over many things in his [936] thoughts, as Paul says: "The married man is concerned for the things of the world, how he will please his wife and he is divided".[30] But you, yourselves, oh wonderful seekers of God, continue to be his undivided ones, always saying that which was earnestly spoken by David: "My soul kept very close, following you, and your right hand upheld me".[31] For you were not driven after fields, houses, or some other thing in order that by laying hold of these things, you might acquire them; neither after irrational desire or slander or the love of money or some other treacherous thing, but as it has been written: "You will follow after the Lord your God and be joined to him".[32] You have truly done this!

"Go, sell your possessions and give to the poor and you will have treasure in heaven, and then follow me".[33] The power of the saying appears in you, which you have not neglected.[34] You have firmly renounced the world and its cares, having greatly taken courage in the divine saying: "Seek first the Kingdom of God and his righteousness and all these things will be given to you".[35]

---

[28] Song 5:1.
[29] Literally "uncultivated" or "undomesticated", providing a direct antinomy with the idea of the monk as a tree cultivated by attention to the law and commandments of God. Antithesis is a favorite rhetorical form used by Sarapion. See his *Letter to Bishop Eudoxius* and his *Against the Manichaeans* for extended examples.
[30] 1 Cor 7:33-34a.
[31] Ps 62:8 (63:8).
[32] Migne cites Deut 10:20 here. However, only the very last portion of the quotation, speaking of being joined to God, seems to fit the LXX text. Sarapion is either quoting a variant from memory, or from a different verse, neither of which I have been unable to find.
[33] Matt 19:21.
[34] Literally, they are "ones who do not overtake/run beyond it". Sarapion is implying that those who adopt the values of the world are those who run forward on their own, seeking their own path, whereas the monks, having renounced worldly values, virtuously follow God and do not try to surpass him. They are content with staying the course. Of course, this is also a means of implicitly reminding the monks that they are to stay the course theologically and ecclesiastically, an implication almost certainly intended by Sarapion, given his status as a bishop and the theological crises of the time.
[35] Matt 6:33.

Wherefore, you are worthy of praises and blessings, having submitted your uninstructed ear to Christ, in order that you might not enslave it to vain slanders. In order that you might teach your eyes not to love other possessions, seeing straight, you practice lifting them to God, saying together with David the hymnographer: "I lifted my eyes to you, who dwell in heaven. Behold, as the eyes of servants look to the hands of their lords, as the eyes of a handmaiden look to the hands of her mistress, so our eyes look to the Lord our God until he has mercy on us".[36] By continually lifting your holy hands to God, you have become accustomed to gaze intently upon God through pure prayers in order that the causes of robberies, thefts, and wars might not come into being. It has been your custom to walk your feet in the right paths, either into the house of God or into the cells of the holy fathers, so that not running toward evil, you will not fall into pits.[37]

For concerning the smell of your freedom, you are accustomed to say to God: "We run toward the odour of your perfume".[38] For you also have acquired the taste for cheap foods; you are satisfied with drinking water, in order not to exaggerate the roles [of food and drink] for the benefit of the stomach and most of all because the deviation came into being by Adam's tasting.[39] Besides all these things, you have also acquired a rough and humble garment, at the same time displaying the way of truth and asceticism. Without transgressions, a rush-mat is pleasant and a blanket is revered (as opposed to a soft mattress with sins). Hearing about the resurrection and the fearful judgment is pleasant to you rather than hearing flutes and stringed instruments and vain songs. A glorious death is chosen by you rather than a prolonged life of luxury.

Therefore you are blessed, most honoured ones! For this is continuously worthy to be said of you: you are the blessed ones [937] who have served the co-essential[40] Trinity. A common man does not deceive a soldier, but neither do the demons, who have fled your piety. For God, who gives gifts to you, said: "Behold, I have given you authority to tread upon serpents and scorpions and

---

[36] Ps 122:1-2 (123:1-2).
[37] Reference to passages such as Rev 20:3 and Sir 21:10 may be intended here.
[38] Song 1:4. Sarapion would seem to be indicating that the monks, by not indulging themselves in expensive perfumes and living plainly in the desert, present an unmasked body odour. Such sentiments may well be difficult to understand in our overly hygienic age with readily available hot showers and cheap perfumes and colognes.
[39] See Gen 3:8, where Adam and Eve eat of fruit of the tree of the knowledge of good and evil. Sarapion interprets this to mean that humanity, through Adam, deviated from God's original plan through an act of self-centred bodily gluttony. It should also be noted that παράβασις can be interpreted not only as "deviation" or "digression", but also "illusion", a likewise valid interpretation here in light of Sarapion's *Treatise Against the Manichees*, where he understands sin to be the result of a mental and spiritual deception.
[40] Sarapion uses ὁμοουσίῳ, clearly referring to Athanasian orthodoxy.

upon all the power of the enemy and nothing will injure you".⁴¹

You have not been enrolled in the army of a human king in order that you might see the slaughter of fellow men in war, but you have been enrolled in the army of Christ in order that you might see the defeat of demons. Nor do you have weapons of copper and iron to kill fellow servants. Rather, you have acquired a strong faith whereby the devil has been overthrown. Furthermore, you have not been enrolled in the army in order that you might pour out human blood, but you have been enrolled in the army of God in order that you might continuously pour out your supplication to his face. "The eyes of the Lord are upon the righteous and his ears are open to their supplication."⁴²

Therefore you prayed on behalf of the world, having known very well that he hears the prayers of the righteous and that the supplication of the righteous man is powerful, working many things.⁴³ You have continually made mention of us.

A paradise of delights will be established for you. And the doors of paradise, which Adam's transgression closed, your desire for God will open. For heaven was established on your behalf, so that you might meet face to face with the apostles, see the prophets, behold the martyrs, embrace all the righteous, spend time with the angels. There you will be blessed and will be more blessed in your life thereafter. There you will see John the Baptiser, the originator of your asceticism, who was nourished in the desert and prominent in his asceticism. There you will see the most courageous Job (a participant in your sufferings and an admirer of your endurance) surrounded with many glories. There you will see your forefather Abraham, who has become a genuine admirer of your hospitality. There the most mild and ascetic David (whose life daily encourages you) will meet you. And, lest the naming of each of the righteous might prolong this letter, you will see Christ himself as the head of all his good people saying: "Blessed are the pure in heart, for they shall see God".⁴⁴ Therefore who is more blessed or happier than you since you will see God with your very own eyes?

You will be blessed on the day of judgment, most desirable ones, when God judges the secrets of men. For all things are naked and have been laid open before his eyes. "For all of us must stand before the judgment seat of Christ so that each might receive recompense for what he did through the body, whether

---

⁴¹ Luke 10:19.
⁴² Ps 33:15 (34:15). Again, it should be noted that the antithesis used in this paragraph comparing the two types of "military" enrolment is characteristic of Sarapion's argumentation. See his *Letter to Bishop Eudoxius* and his *Against the Manichaeans* for extended examples.
⁴³ Jas 5:16.
⁴⁴ Matt 5:8.

good or evil."[45] Trembling will not seize you at that time, but merriment and joy and a crown of exaltation in the Holy Spirit. Neither the judgment nor the fire of the ages,[46] nor the worm that never sleeps,[47] will be fearful to you, but to the ones who act contrary and transgress God's decree.

You hear this: "Come, blessed ones of my Father, inherit the kingdom prepared for you from the foundation of the world",[48] you who have constantly understood the things of Christ. But against the common enemy of all [940], and against the ones who followed him, that awe-inspiring saying will say: "Let the ungodly one be taken away, so that he might not see the glory of the Lord".[49] You will go forth with merriment and joy to where grief and pain and sighing have fled,[50] where honour and glory and graces are irremovable.

For your piety is celebrated everywhere throughout the entire inhabited world. What kind of city, having heard of your virtuous and apostolic life, does not pray to see you? What king previously, or even at this present time, hearing of your venerable and virtuous life, has not sought to consult you and embrace you with great affection? From you has come forth Father Anthony, on account of the highest life, whose written *Life* is also preserved among you. So, too, Father Amoun, Father John, and Father Macarius, who have valiantly shone forth in pre-eminence, and who have displayed both miracles and other powerful signs to men, by having expelled demons in accordance with the will of God, and by having cured great pains of diseases and other kinds of sufferings. They exhibited the weakness of physicians. For the sufferings that the physicians were not able to heal, the physicians conceded were healed by their holy prayers and strong faith, acknowledging their own proper methods and their limits to heal. Hearing these things, kings marvelled, enthusiastically praising God.

You know these things more accurately than we do. For you have spent time with them and so have your fathers. Therefore, who will be able to declare your praises worthily? Who will not approve or commend your love of God, patience, intelligence, and purity, along with your prudence,

---

[45] 2 Cor 5:10.
[46] Matt 18:8 and especially Mark 9:43.
[47] Sarapion here either has a different text of Isaiah and/or Mark or is making an interpretation. Isa 66:24 and Mark 9:48, as we have them, speak of the worm that never ends or completes, that is, that never dies. There is a subtle distinction between a reference to a symbolic punishment of hell that never ends versus one that never sleeps. The notion of a worm that never sleeps is less contrary to Sarapion's belief in a finite hell, which serves a corrective function. Even if the worm symbolises a creature, rather than punishment(s), then the text as we have it is not problematic as even the "worm" could eventually be corrected. On this note, see sections 29 and 30 of his *Against the Manichaeans*.
[48] Matt 25:34.
[49] Isa 26:10.
[50] Isa 35:10.

gentleness and silence, civilised manners, peacefulness, absence of pretence, and straightforwardness, dispassion, unselfishness, tenderheartedness, compassion, generosity, sympathy, brotherly love and hospitality, love toward beggars, friendliness in conversation, love of truth, single-mindedness with respect to God, your words, sweet as honey, your soft speech, your sure-footedness, solitude, outstanding fame, orthodoxy, and faith in God?

Oh, with how much virtue have you lived! Oh, how much virtue surrounds you, men most honoured by God! Oh, from how many virtues do you wear a crown! Much tranquillity is among you because of good works! Peace rules over you because of the abstinence from evil things. Over you rules humility, a true type of the Lord, by which the Devil, having missed the mark from the beginning, has been justly overthrown.

It was necessary and most proper to write and say these things to you, for it has been written: "The memory of the righteous is thereafter praised".[51] For the people [941] will be gladdened when the righteous ones are praised.[52] Therefore, when anyone remembers you, he also certainly applies praise to you. Therefore, most courageous men, because you clearly acknowledge your dignity and glory, you have prevailed in perfecting your reward by being increasingly vigilant because of the hope of things to come and by singing David's phrase: "Take courage! Let your heart be strengthened and wait on the Lord".[53]

May some other view never bring all this to ruin. Nor, after so much time, may some slight heedlessness regarding the things good for your soul extinguish your brilliant lights, a wind blowing in the opposite direction, since you appear as lights of heaven shining in the world, in order that you might hear, together with the apostles: "You are the light of the world",[54] and also the Apostle saying: "You have need of endurance so that, having done the will of God, you might honour his promise".[55]

So, do not grow weary, most honoured men, but connect the end to the beginning and the beginning to the end. "For the one who endures to the end—this one—will be saved."[56] May it come to pass that you and we, who are nourished by divine dogmas, ruled by God, and shepherded by him, attain a blessed and holy end, having been trained for it so that having succeeded, we might boldly say those prayerful words spoken by the Apostle: "I have fought the good fight. I have completed the race. I have kept faith. From now on, there

---

[51] Prov 10:7.
[52] Prov 29:2.
[53] Ps 26:14 (27:14).
[54] Matt 5:14.
[55] Heb 10:36. Migne offers κομίσησθε, the verb also given in the critical Greek text edited by Aland and others, for κοσμήσησθε, the verb in the text. I have chosen to interpret the verb given in the text of the letter (κοσμήσησθε).
[56] Matt 24:13.

is reserved for me a crown of righteousness, which the Lord, the righteous judge, will give to me on that day".⁵⁷

Glory and power to the Father, and to the Son, and to the Holy Spirit unto the ages of ages! Amen!

---
⁵⁷ 2 Tim 4:7-8.

Against the Manichaeans*

1
Truth refutes error and destroys deceit, and does not permit any falsehood to proceed. Let us entreat the Lord Jesus, who is Truth, to enlighten our mind so that deceit may not be able to capture our mind nor error be strong enough to conquer, and, if they have captured and conquered, that they may not have lasting dominion. For only by enlightening and shining the beams of his Truth will one disperse the deceit that has occurred and maintain the mind undeceived. For he himself cries out: "I am the way, and the Truth, and the life",[1] he himself commanding: "Be on guard against those false prophets who are coming to you in sheep's clothing but inside are ravenous wolves".[2] For since their manner was a deceptive appearance and their disposition fabricated, Truth did not remain silent, but revealed himself,[3] not permitting what was hidden in the mind to be covered by what was fabricated and formed in pretence, so that their deceit, made manifest, might be made weak in their attacks and capable of seizing no one.

2
Evil, therefore, is diverse and multiform, having exposed its attacks in various ways, some of its parts more hurtful and destructive than others. Therefore neither the smaller things are to be passed over in silence, nor the greater things left alone, since we know this: that the lesser portions of evil do less harm and the greater do greater harm. For the one who has fallen in greater matters has also received greater punishment, and the one who has been deceived by greater things is also corrected more strongly. For the deceits are measured, but the faults are also measured and, being weighed on the scale by the judge, the punishment is exacted. For he has spoken: "Who has measured heaven with a span and the earth with a hand's breadth? Who has weighed the mountains with a scale and the forests with a balance beam?"[4] He permits no imbalance, but measuring it out, he prescribes the punishment according to the deceit of each deceiver and the temper of the one who has been cheated. Therefore we must be zealous not to be persuaded by the smallest deceit. For even the smallest deceit, having taken hold of the consent of the soul, like a spark thrown on firewood, ignites and produces a great fire. For many who

---

* Text translated from Casey, *Serapion of Thmuis*, 29-78.
[1] John 14:6.
[2] Matt 7:15.
[3] One could also render this passage something along the lines of: "Truth did not remain silent, but revealed/laid bare [the facts of the matter]". I have chosen a christocentric rendering.
[4] Isa 40:12.

began from a small deceit have been led into a flood of deceit.

3
On account of this, we must be careful not to be persuaded by the smallest deceit, building a most favourable wall for the soul, so that we are not persuaded by the greater ones. For the one who has fallen because of the smallest will also be deceived with respect to the greater, and the one who has been persuaded by none of the small ones will have undeniable steadfastness even against the great ones.

Since, therefore, many wolves (clothed in the fleeces of sheep) have come forward, let the shepherd's knowledge not be kept secret, but let him shake the sword of the Word, warding off danger for the nurslings and fighting on behalf of the flock striving for the security for the flock, but also revealing the attack of the wild animals. For behold! There are many who have come forward and they wander here and there, having worn the name of Christ (in the place of fleeces) and calling themselves something they are not (but being something they refuse to be called). Hiding their own evil behind the dignity of the name and uniting with the name, but striving to destroy completely the name of Christ, they fight against Jesus while calling upon Jesus! For this is the most dangerous evil, because they say the name of Christ while fighting Christ. For since evil was too weak to war against God, it has borrowed the name, in order that having persuaded the thoughts of the senseless by the use of the name, as if the name of Christ were its own (as it pretends here and there), it might mistreat the ones who have believed in the Saviour. In this way, Valentinus came forth, as did Marcion and Sitanus and, from another place, Ophanius. The last miscarriage of evil, the insanity of Mani, came forth, having diminished all the other evils and, by a greater evil, exhibited the other evils as second-rate. Besides, in the prophetic writings it is written: "On account of the complete neglect of Jerusalem, Sodom has been justified because of you".[5] Many wicked teachings that have been deceiving have corresponded with the enormity of the false teachings of the Manichaeans, and are presently being flooded by a sea of evil.

4
In order that we might not argue with the wicked inconsistently, might not think we succeed at providing a proof against their faults (which bear against the exact reason we might put forth) by saying only their names, and so that we might destroy their deceptions, let us persuade them into the midst of Truth.

Evil is without essence and without a sure foundation. Rather, action is its "essence" and it is an action of free will corresponding to those who are sick

---
[5] Ezek 16:52.

with respect to their free will. Moreover, it is an action that has joined (but is easily removed from) those who are sick. When it has been joined and is no longer separated, it might be said that evil does not exist on its own but that that essence can never exist without evil. If the essence had free will from before that joining occurred, however, then the evil is easily removed, so that, in turn, the purity that lies beneath is restored and it does not even have the sign of evil. Evil will not exist on its own, nor is it able always to exist, but is being destroyed and refuted by extermination, and is not able simply to exist nor did it exist at some time, but recently has come forth from a sickened free will.

5

Words and actions testify that it is not possible to see the soul as essentially good in itself, with regard to how it has been produced and exists nor the body as something essentially evil in itself. For if self-control is a virtue, but the body essentially evil, the body would not be found self-controlled because the body, which would be essentially disgraceful, would not become virtuous. For when the body is self-controlled, the body has become virtuous, and the body is virtuous, and because the body is virtuous, it can even be a temple. If, therefore, every body was impure and it was impossible for self-control to be found in bodies, we would have been able to ascribe an essential evil to the essence of bodies. But if the body has advanced so far and has been so honoured, and has put on so much temperance, so as to be a house for the one who created it and a treasury for the Lord, so that the Father and Son dwell in and receive the residence of bodies, how is their reasoning not absurd and laughable?

6

For behold! Somewhere Paul says: "Do you not know that your bodies are a temple of the Holy Spirit in you?"[6] God promised through the prophet: "I will dwell in them and I will move among them and I will be their God".[7] He both persuades the mind, and witnesses to the body. And what is "essential" he expels, whereas striving restores actions. For when striving restores what is suitable to daily life, then such a preparation is restored in the bodies, so that bodies too are able to serve the spirit and reason.[8]

So, how is the tongue able to serve the things that have been thought? For if the tongue is evil in essence, but the mind good, how is the tongue able to participate in the things that have been thought (the thought being brought to light through the explanation)? For just as no self-control is produced from

---

[6] 1 Cor 6:19.
[7] 2 Cor 6:16 ; cf. Lev 26:12.
[8] Casey's text notes a lacuna in the text between "what is essential", (   ) and "he expels" (   ).

fornication, so it is not possible for something genuine to proceed from that which is essentially evil. Therefore, when one inspects every part—the ear, the eyes, the tongue, the other parts—and sees that they have been produced as instruments of learning, then he will accept the body and not blame it and he will see these works of creation as pure, and loathe the hated deceiver of truth.

7

If some of the bodies always were self-controlled, not ever heedless, but some were always heedless, not restrained by self-control even in part, it could be said that a division had occurred among the bodies and some were produced self-controlled and some heedless. However, their argument was weak on this point. For reason was no longer present with them, against all bodies, if they declared such a hypothesis, but the refutation was easily satisfied. How is it possible, since bodies have the same essence, to conceive of two opposed natures from the same essence and to divide the same essence into two natures, so that one part is always evil and the other always good, and so that they are not accepting of themselves but fighting against themselves, annihilating themselves, destroying themselves in struggle since the same substance never fights against itself or annihilates itself, and their premise will again be shown to be nonsense and foolishness after these demonstrations are produced.

8

If bodies are not so, not always self-controlled or always heedless, but there is fear concerning the self-controlled that they might ever be heedless through negligence (for already many of the bodies exhibiting self-control have been overtaken and absorbed through the passion of desires), there is hope concerning the wanton and undisciplined bodies, because already many of the bodies that were heedless have advanced so greatly in self-control, so as that they do not even have signs of many intemperate things, that they are freed, through improvement and great advancement from all "wrinkle and spot" of old.[9] Therefore, when the Gospel says: "the tax collectors and the prostitutes are going before you into heaven", when Paul says: "by faith, Rahab the prostitute was not destroyed together with those who were disobedient",[10] from what essence or nature were the bodies? For if they were of a good nature, how were they heedless? And if they were of an evil nature, how has the nature been self-controlled? But if nature had changed from heedlessness into self-control and was at some point heedless but at another self-controlled, and was able to act heedlessly, and yet was able to be self-controlled after acting heedlessly (as the changes demonstrate), nature has been freed, free will has been observed, and

---

[9] Eph 5:27.
[10] Heb 11:31.

the body is no longer essentially evil, but serves the free will and is a servant subject to free will, not nature, and it will become whatever free will might make it.

9

For when the mind, having ascertained understanding, should come to a desire of understanding, then even the body, having been freed from provocative emotions, honours steadfastness and does not oppose the assistance of actions. But whenever negligence and vanity pervert the understanding (that is to say, whenever weakness and vanity are produced by the mind), then passion is inscribed on the body and is revealed as being nothing other than a boundary between them.

What is written is true. "Behold, I have set before you death and life. Choose what you wish."[11] This is so that the agent who makes the decision may request righteous judgment and not have constraint and compulsion upon his actions as some forced defence. So he is not naturally a blameless person, being unable to fight against nature, but having a choice between the two, being the master of the determinations of his own judgment, he may demand critical examinations and defences. For what he chose, he chose freely, and therefore he is judged for what was done voluntarily, since he committed these actions through his own choice. If this were not so, the saints were crowned in vain. Also the evil were tormented on account of folly if the culpability of an action was not ascribed to the doers of the action.

10

Therefore what has impelled the Manichaeans to being slander against bodies, since they are denounced by the Scriptures and ancient oracles? For self-control, being an act, testifies to a self-controlled body and the oracles, shouting and saying: "Present your bodies as a living sacrifice, acceptable to God",[12] make sufficient proof. For God neither accepts what is not his own nor demands what has been created by another, so that he himself might not become violent, demanding violence against others, and so that he might not covet something belonging to another, as if he could not create it himself. For if it is honourable, and he wishes bodies to be self-controlled, how could he not make what he wished? But if he himself has not made the body (with the result that it might be naturally evil), how did it change its nature so that it no longer has its own and is not evil, but holy? And if a nature can be changed, how is it still a nature, being transformed and becoming the opposite of itself? For what receives transformation and change no longer receives the definition "nature".

---

[11] Jer 21:8. See also Deut 30:19.
[12] Rom 12:1.

The body changes and transforms and is easily self-controlled. The words shout: "you shall not fornicate", crying out: "you shall not commit adultery",[13] allowing abrogation by being precepts and refusal by being exhortations that can be accomplished and giving reason as an ally to the mind, so that the intellect tending toward virtue, may draw the body toward virtue.

11

The bodies of the saints, of course, have advanced so much so as to be honoured and not made empty of either divine energies or divine powers. The body of Elisha lay dead and, lying dead, raised the dead.[14] It scared away death, freed the one who had died, sent the one who had died back to the living, provided an awakening for the one who had fallen asleep. If the Manichaeans have been angry with this, even resenting the oracle and not honouring the Law, let them be shamed by a parallel example let the shadow of Peter shame their minds. For the shadow was of Peter's body and, having been cast over the sickened bodies, produced bodies free from illnesses.[15]

12

Since there are so many demonstrative words and so many demonstrative actions, how would the ones who had made haste to join contradictory things not be wrong in the expression of their words? For the Manichaeans declare:

> We have borne the body of Satan, but the soul is from God. Thus the body is naturally evil, having come from evil, but the soul is naturally good, having its origin from good. Therefore, there are two principles and two essences. Two principles have produced two responsible causes: one an evil body and the other a good soul. Therefore the soul is good and the body is evil.

But how is the body self-controlled and the soul often heedless? And how is it that each of them does not remain in its proper place, but often the body is self-controlled and often the soul is heedless? A reversal has occurred. What had been "from the Devil" is now "from God" and what had been "from God" is now "from the Devil", and the often-babbled hostility has been destroyed, and a truce and friendship have occurred, God sending the soul to the Devil and the Devil sending the body back to God to serve him. For the self-controlled[16] body serves God but what is "from God" is able to serve the Devil,

---

[13] Exod 20:13, 14.
[14] 4 Kgs 13:21.
[15] Acts 5:15.
[16] Casey notes a lacuna at this point. Fitschen structures these last couple of lines from section 12 so as to say the sober-minded ("self-controlled") body is what belongs to God but still serves the Devil, thus emphasizing the reversal or irony that Sarapion notes. I have tried to fill in the lacuna and keep the Greek words in such a way as to flow a little better with

for the unbelieving person and the one who utters blasphemies serve the Devil.

13

Therefore how is it not proper that the sensible are laughing excessively and greatly deriding those who have worked hard to introduce such absurd and ridiculous dogmas? That reason itself has been grasped even by the senseless, who have been able to leave behind again the chosen senselessness and do leave it behind, the affairs of the youngest son are sufficient proof.[17] Through heedlessness toward his father, he left his father, started a long journey into the passions, and lived in wastefulness. After a long time, he laid hold of himself, turns back, and returns to his father. He gets rid of the shameful things. He goes forward begging. He obtains forgiveness. For the beginning of lessons learned, which came about with much cost, expunged the lamentation of sin and brought about a reasonable and divine feast.

14

I do not know if they slander the Apostle or reckon him among the apostles on account of his later deeds. For if they slander him on account of the earlier things he did, what will they say concerning the later? If they commend the later things, what do they say about the earlier things? For the former things are not in harmony with the later things.

He was a wolf but was found to be a shepherd. He was a destroyer but today is a shield as a protector. He has deliberately chosen to pour out the blood of the flock but, at the end he is daring, and hastened to pour out his own blood. For having been born just now and having gone through the birth pangs of a mother even until the hour of death, he did not live continuously as he was but suffered diverse changes and transitions, having found the auspicious goal and, by means of recanting, proclaimed the new way of life. Of course, he did not blush, and did not keep the earlier things secret. He is the one who has enacted the honour of the new life because he has passed through so many disparaging things, has ascended to such a great height of virtue, and cried: "For this Jesus Christ came into the world: to save sinners, of whom I am first. Because of this I received mercy, in order that Jesus might exhibit, in me, his entire forbearance as an example for those who will believe".[18]

15

When we have beheld the chorus of the apostles, we will know about sinful and profane men, and those who fell many times long ago and are no longer

---

Sarapion's emphasis on free will. However, this does not diametrically oppose Fitschen's rendering.
[17] Luke 15.11-32.
[18] 1 Tim 1:15.

possess two things: the act of falling many times and the act of no longer falling. Therefore, if they were of an evil nature, they would have always been falling, but if they were of a good nature, they never would have fallen.

But if the ones who fell many times and sinned greatly have come not to sin, and came to live unfalteringly, the definition of the soul is revealed to be self-secure and acting in free will. By nature, it is not oriented toward anything, but producing change by free will and turning wherever it wills and turning back again, wherever it chooses, spending time here, and then spending time there and there, as it wills, making its will the standard for its action. For the will of the one who does the deed happens to be the standard for the action.

But if they have loved what they have hated and have hated what they have loved and the mind has not remained in hate, but lightly moves about like a bird, wherever it desires, where is "nature"? For it is necessary that the nature that always hates hates what is hated and the nature that always loves loves what is loved. It can in no way love what is hated or hate what is loved. For where minds change and where so many preferences assume such changes, how would the action not be a struggle?

16

At one time Jesus was hated by Paul, but then he was very much loved by the one who hated him.[19] The robber's life was loved by the robber and virtue was hated. And his mind changed so much that he loved beyond all measure what was altogether hated.

For this is peculiar to what is virtuous — to love what was hated and to hate what was loved. Many, being young, used to love the shameful things and hated holy things. And today, having come into knowledge, they have been set apart for holy purposes. Through this they are not recognised. Through this they struggled against themselves. Through this they do not accept the old likeness and yet they are truly men. They did not cease to be men. While nature remains permanent, the ways of living do not remain permanent. Natures have not been destroyed but ways of life have been completely destroyed. The nature of each, human nature, stands firm.

But I should no longer explain the man. He was immoral and became self-controlled. He was thievish but has come to represent the charitable life. He has not destroyed the character of his person. The character of the dignity remains. He did not eliminate the dignity of his nature.

17

When I behold a man, I observe of what nature he is, but when I behold the way he lives, I am astonished! I no longer recognise him. The change in behaviour

---

[19] Acts 9:1-20 and Gal 1:13-17.

has presented to me the effect of the change in him. However, our natures have not changed since the body remains a body, not having become something else. Neither has the body been turned into an immaterial thing nor did the soul begin to exist as another thing by nature. But while the natures remain the same, the ways of living did not remain the same.

18

Therefore what shall we say? If the ways of living did not remain the same while the natures remain the same, the ways of living are no longer essential. For if the ways of living remained together with their natures, they would not change. If the natures have remained the same and the ways of living have not remained the same, then certainly the eye that was previously overpowered by desire has self-control as a security key. Also the tongue that was previously hasty and rash and rattled on before making discernments now is persuaded by restraint and having changed its habits, is now at rest. It moderated itself and henceforth is self-controlled.

Desire was not the nature of the eye nor was indiscretion the nature of the tongue, nor was heedlessness the nature of the body. If it is necessary to pay attention to things pertaining to nature, one should not keep silent about these things — the nature of the eye was the act of seeing, not how it saw, and the nature of the tongue was the act of speaking, not how it spoke. For the quality of the movements is dependent on the free will. The simple and safe movement of the actions has been assigned to parts of the body. Therefore the simple movement is safe, but change is uncertain. When the intelligence and understanding lead the eyes, sight is right and godly so long as it is prostrate before worthy things, but when heedlessness reigns, the actions are shameful and adulterated.

Thus the body (and each part) honours the action and imitates the action. What has been made is beautiful, for it is able to serve virtue. The laws are holy for they manage the care of that which has been made. Mix the Law with what is created and you will see that what has been made is similar to Creator and it will emulate the Creator. However, if you have creation but you do not render the laws (being the image impressed on creation) to the creation, you dare to speak against it with slander. Resolving to treat creation with contempt, you work lawless violence against the Creator.

19

Since also in the soul, there is some essential existence and its essential existence has not been destroyed nor will it be destroyed, ways of living have often been destroyed and can be destroyed. Why do you define as not being capable of being destroyed what is able to be destroyed in essence? There are often souls which had been seized by senselessness which later bound fast to prudence and often, appearing prominent in prudence, at a later time have fallen into senselessness. You have often heard: "while a man was in high esteem, he did not understand. He was comparable to the mindless cattle and was like them".[20] And Paul cried out: "God chose the foolish things in the world in order that he might shame the wise".[21] Therefore those who belonged to the foolish have come upon prudence and those who belonged to the prudent have come upon foolishness, and heedlessness seized the mind, prudence having been overtaken by sickness, but seizing the senseless mind, instruction recovered it, having forced the sickness out of the senseless mind and restored health as the mistress of the house.

Therefore evils and virtues exchanged places. They are both acquired and lost. You have, you do not have. You have found and you have lost. You have what you found. You do not have what you lost. Judge between things that are found or lost. One is what has been found and the other is what has been lost. One is virtue and one is contrived. One is evil and one is what is practised. And the one that is evil is nothing, for in itself it is nothing.

For it is impossible to find the essential existence of evil. Rather, evil receives activity, of course, from the understanding and emotions through vanity of a conceived thought and care for a course of action undertaken from emotions. Examine the exterior! Contemplate the interior! Know your thoughts well whenever you endure disorder, some confusion, or whenever some pleasure entices. In this way, whenever still in danger, by bringing in a little instruction, you might perceive calm in the soul and much tranquillity, and these things happen in this way – with not a lot of time having passed, but often in a moment such a thing occurs.

20

And since the soul often rushes toward shameful passion, but immediately humbles itself and quietens down and again knows self-control, and since such a thing as this takes place, how is it possible not to receive this as a marvel? How can one not say that nothing is proper to it, but the soul appropriates, having been appropriated from what it wishes? And nothing from what is shameful exists because of itself, but seems to exist when it appears in thought. Therefore shameful activities do not exist because of themselves, but with favourably disposed and backsliding thoughts they accept their formation. Because of this the soul required schools, receiving sharpening and brilliance from schools. For this reason, it often speaks loudly to itself, arousing itself; or, being aroused by another, it hears: "my soul praises the Lord and all that is within me praises

---

[20] Ps 48:20 (49:20).
[21] 1 Cor 1:27.

his holy name"[22], and: "my soul glorifies the Lord".[23] For either the arousing and restoring words have prepared it to be yet more courageous or the things coming to pass (because of the exhortation) give it a perfect state of being. But often it also arouses itself for what is shameful and makes room in itself for an exhortation and gives itself harmful things, cries out: "Soul, you have goods laid up for many years. Eat! Drink! Be merry!"[24]

21

And if the souls providing harmful things for themselves were other kinds of souls and they were together with yet others but others that, in another manner, had things pertaining to self-control, one could say there were two kinds of souls. And while saying this, one necessarily derides and shames the absurd opinion of the Manichaeans, because in their insanity they cut and divide in two both by proclaiming things fighting against themselves and by not instilling respect for unanimity with their absurd opinion. But if souls are the same, and at one time the soul that has recommended to itself the absurd things should then recommend to itself the honourable things, and the soul that at one time arouses holy things in itself should then send forth shameful things to itself, and the soul that formerly has sought after holy things and honoured holy things later has left them behind, free choice will have been tested by the change.

22

While Demas was with Paul, honouring the Pauline community, he was seized by the desire for the Devil, left the apostolic communion and, becoming one who flees, he hurried after worldly glory. "Demas has left me, having loved the present age, and gone to Thessalonika".[25] Formerly Gehazi followed Elisha and travelled in his service. But when an opportunity for wealth appeared, he left divine activities and, receiving money, he sold his own mind in return for the obtaining of wealth.[26] Judas, being among the apostles, once drove out a fever, led an army against demons, was one of the ones saying: "Lord, behold! Even the demons are subject to us!"[27] And the one who urged on the scourge against the demons having been grasped by a small sickness, was enticed by desire. Therefore people such as these changed from so great a participation to a shameful existence.

---

[22] Ps 102:1 (103:1).
[23] Ps 145:1 (146:1).
[24] Luke 12:19.
[25] 2 Tim 4:10.
[26] 4 Kgs 5:20.
[27] Luke 10:17. The "army" is a reference to the seventy apostles.

23

But what does one say concerning Peter or Thomas? That once he was a fisherman and a bad person. For he was not unerring, but was a man. And having been called, he left the drag-nets and the fish and, having discarded everything, he followed in order that he might have only Jesus. Leaving the things of his former life, he was not deprived of what he desired. For he found what he sought, and has advanced to such a state of mind so as to hear: "You are Simon the son of Jonah. You will be called Cephas, which is translated Peter".[28] He heard: "I will give to you, Peter, the keys of the kingdom of heaven".[29] He received the testimony: "Flesh and blood did not reveal this to you, but my Father who is in heaven".[30]

Later, he was seized by a reckless saying and coming to the penalty, and not fleeing the penalty, he heard: "Get behind me Satan! You are an offence to me because you do not understand the things of God but the things of men".[31] And he had just received the keys of heaven since the Father uttered through Jesus "Peter" instead of "Simon" but instead received a reprimand for his action. But the error was healed by improvement and the penalty became a cure. And Peter's mind held onto the healing and he was great and divine, having healed the error and having been damaged because of what was said before.

But when the Lord was handed over and led into the court of the high priest, the vigorous Peter was disgraced and ashamed. The one having the keys trembled! He dared to speak truth outside the gates of truth! He who had been satisfied emptied his mind. He is conquered by one servant woman. He fears a young girl. He is not able to look into the face of a slave. The God-fearing man, the man loved by God, the one knowing the revealed things, the eyewitness of the Lord, falls because of cowardice. And I do not say these things in order that I might denounce him. It is because he trusts that I may say these things; so that the truth might not be slandered. I speak loudly on the behalf of truth. I exhibit the servant of truth so that falsehood might not prevail. I bring forth the servant of truth.

Because they want natures to be otherwise and they are furious over the principle of nature,[32] I have brought forth Peter in order that nature might be examined. For the many changes demonstrate what is produced by free will. And their murmuring will be fruitless when free will achieves favourable verdicts through judgment. For we live by free will, it is by free will that we attain virtuous action.

---

[28] John 1:42.
[29] Matt 16:19.
[30] Matt 16:17.
[31] Matt 16:23.
[32] That is, that free will is the guiding quality of a nature.

24

Therefore I am afraid lest we might not be persuaded. We always toil against something careless so that we might not unexpectedly fall into ruin through carelessness, thinking we are secure. For our sake, Paul says: "I punish and enslave my body so that, having proclaimed to others, I might never become reprobate myself".[33] I fear this saying regarding reprobation. Knowing the slipperiness of free will, I secure myself against something easy through carefulness. I fortify the laxity of free will by the suffering toil of care. And Peter says and writes and rejoices in these things so that his errors and his virtuous acts may produce an introduction into the teachings. For this reason, the sins of the saints are also spoken of. For what error did harm in silence in order to be kept secret?

Who is the one writing? For evil men did not speak against good men, but good men spoke at length about the errors of good men, and others, their own errors – Paul of his own errors and John (of Peter's errors and then Thomas'), one the errors of another. For if the evil men were the ones who spoke against them, we would dispute with the hater and find fault with the ill-will and slander because such words were uttered from ones who hate. Since, however, the same men spoke against their own errors or good men spoke of the accusations against good men (though actually the Holy Spirit is the one who spoke through the saints), and the Lord himself told at length the errors of his own servants and has not kept silent, we seek the cause of this. For it was not spoken in order that they might be discredited, for they removed the discredit, but in order that the blameless ones might not conjecture a nature consisting of sins that have been kept secret. Therefore the argument is on behalf of truth and the narration of the errors introduce truth.

25

O what unprecedented wonder! The sins of saints have been written in order that the truth might be made known, because having produced from similar natures and, in like manner, having produced by means of virtue, they received what is greater, not having prevailed by means of nature, but having become prominent through virtue.

But if, in the judgment of Peter and the other apostles, nature does not guide what defines, but free will, with whom do we find unerring nature when we do not find it among the apostles? Where would we be able to seek it out? In vain we investigate things that do not exist. See, I ask Peter. See, I inspect Thomas. I do not speak of the ancient things. I do not bring David to mind. And, indeed, I ought to bring these things to mind so that when those who are ignorant declare from them, they might receive reprimands so that learning

---

[33] 1 Cor 9:27.

from them, they might endure the cross-examination.

For although the Gospels were studied by them, the cross-examination from the Gospels has not been brought before them. On account of this, they speak a lawless reasoning, not having learned. And on account of this, they do not have knowledge of the Gospel, not having received the beginning of the Gospels: "The beginning of the Gospel of Jesus Christ, as it is written in Isaiah the prophet".[34] They spurned the beginning of the lessons. They fought against the beginning of the lessons. They sought the perfected things but were not able to find them, not having accepted what was heard from the beginning.

26

On the one hand, these things are insignificant and few, but on the other hand, they are sufficient for the investigation. For I called forth the only fundamental thing and did not condescend to a plethora of testimonies. For with respect to things similar to the things being said, the reader will investigate and advance from such matters to similar and related readings.

But come, let us construct their reasoning by providing their dogmas.

Satan was evil but God was good. Thus it was. I overturn the myth to put their myth to shame. Besides, if I do not provide what they are expounding, I do not have the means to put to shame the one who has invented the myth. They say God was good but Satan evil. He was evil and there was not a time when he was not. For he always was and was not from someone else. He was, and he was a root cause, they say. And there was a Lord, himself good and a root cause, a good root cause, and a root cause of good things and everything good came from him. For there were two root causes and two emanations came forth (the emanations corresponding to the root causes). They repeatedly babble that similar matters of this kind are from that and other similar matters are from this. We take up these arguments while we undertake a further investigation and consider logical arguments, and we remember the things they stated so that we might both gather together logical arguments and persuade them by means of the things that are said.

For we shall say to them: since God was a root cause, and a good root cause, and good fruits were produced from good root causes, and Satan was a root cause, and an evil root cause, and evil fruits were produced by an evil root cause, from whom were the apostles' fruits? I thus apprehend from root causes, so that we might know what is sought from the fruits. For we will say: the evil root cause did not know how to bring forth good, nor did the good root cause know how to bring forth evil, but the apostles appear at one point good and at another bad and they were later good but formerly bad, having made the change away from bad things. For if we say the apostles are the fruits of Satan

---
[34] Mark 1:1.

on account of former errors, they will be regarded shamefully with respect to apostleship and perfection of virtues. But if we say they are of God, what will they say concerning their former errors and past calumny? For the Scriptures will put them to shame and disprove their judgment.

27

If, being at a loss and unable to speak, they in turn question, asserting the solution of the problems to be difficult and the exposition to be difficult, we will say the apostles are not fruits of God, but are made and formed by him. For they have not been produced as fruits from a root cause, but, as creatures and things made by a creator and maker, they have come into being from the one who made them, not as co-essential with the one who made them. For the originated ones are from the unoriginate God because there was a time when they were not but they were created later, receiving existence from the one who made them, not being essences from an essence, but having been made *hypostases* from the goodness of the divine Craftsman, and thus they were made so that they might possess free will from the beginning.

Therefore the Saviour reveals this by saying: "If someone wishes to come after me",[35] "If you wish to become perfect",[36] and "If you wish to become healthy".[37] If the one calls who has made such things (through whom the Father made all things), then one perceives the utterances of the one who had made such things. He established the laws while willing, he keeps the things conformable to the laws in the faculty of the will, and he establishes the will of the ones acting as the authority over the things being enacted. Most certainly the Word, honouring the common enterprise of actions, made it dependent on the will: "If you are willing and you obey me, you will eat the good things of the earth, but if you are not willing and do not obey me, a sword will devour you".[38]

But it would be inappropriate to omit the account concerning the worst men and to pass over the scrutiny concerning those who behave shamefully and luxuriously, lest in any way our silence might make a most grievous insanity among them. Do they not most certainly misrepresent Nebuchadnezzar? Do they not most certainly censure Pharaoh? Have they not believed them because of their extremely filthy conduct? For they babble such things back and forth concerning their way of life.

If, therefore, no good zeal should appear in their thoughts, there would be another reason. But if in such bad men even portions of good are found (such as perception, apprehension, repentance, and supplications), what will

---
[35] Matt 16:24.
[36] Matt 19:21.
[37] John 5:6.
[38] Isa 1:19, 21.

they say then? For if this entirely shameful situation should reveal something having a share of virtue and kindness in behaviours, what will they say? For they will either say that Satan is composed of virtue and evil (as one bearing mixed fruits) or that these fruits are not of the Devil. For the mixed things would no longer be fruits of the unmixed one and the unmixed one will not be revealed as the root cause of the mixed. But these men were revealed as mixed men, during the course of time having grasped understanding and having been grasped by wickedness. And it will be revealed according to this reasoning: that *hypostases* are creations of the Word and not emanations from truth.

28

Look! Pharaoh gives in to punishments and is softened. He gives in by means of his intellect and, having beaten his breast,[39] he does not remain in a state of harshness but does two things. He asks for prayer[40] and denounces what has occurred. And so the soul is not shown to be helpless, but considering and progressing toward repentance, being receptive to both requests and supplications and persevering to the point of prayer. If the soul had been made evil, how did it discern with regard to prayer and repentance? For if repentance is good and prayer is good but the nature is evil, how was what is evil mixed with what is good? How was something good produced from something evil? They reveal that they do not know what they are saying, but with an uneducated mind they are alleging things more venomous than the words themselves.

Besides, Nebuchadnezzar was also a harsh man in disposition, having made the furnace ready and made the golden image and terrifying them with threats and compelling them to worship the statue, so that the holy ones were thrown into the furnace. Yet the fire recoiled and did not touch their bodies and the furnace became a synagogue and instead of lamentations, hymns of praise were performed in there, and no longer was a funeral-song for a burned body, but a song was performed from a celebrating soul. Nebuchadnezzar stooped to see the things inside, saw the sight of the angel, and emitted a cry. "Did we not cast three men into the furnace? Behold! I see four and the fourth is like a Son of God."[41] Straightaway he wrote a law on behalf of this in order to confess God, to testify to the truth. He became the interpreter of his vision.

Therefore do we reprove or commend the interpretation? Is it good to be an ambassador on behalf of Christ[42] or should we suffer the same for a portion of evil? For if to be an ambassador of the divine oracles and to be a witness for truth is good, and Nebuchadnezzar served as an ambassador and wrote

---

[39] Literally, "having crushed his soul"; κατατυφεὶς τὴν ψυχήν
[40] Exod 10:16-17.
[41] Dan 3:24-25.
[42] 2 Cor 5:20.

his decree and sent it forth to each of his magistrates, nature had been freed. For knowing the good, he perceived the knowledge of what was good. If he had dulled the knowledge because of his disposition toward evil, he would be accused. It is one thing not to be wholly able to do good, but another to perceive what is good and not be able to do it, being weakened because of an inclination toward passion.

29

But since the fruits of the Devil have not been found among men and yet their way of life was put to shame and their absurdity refuted, to where should we direct our attention further? Unless we immediately proceed to the demons, they will surely say: "Not one fruit of the Devil exists in men, but only demons, his children and offspring", and while saying these things, they will be put to shame. Because of this, they should listen first. If up to this time not one man has been loosed from the One, therefore having nothing in common with Satan and this life, but rather, he has released himself from all things, has become a stranger to all things, then he has departed from knowledge, having become one expelled from teaching.

But if you desire to learn that the demons themselves are not evil from their root cause, and do not have a wicked root cause, but that they have arrived at this because of free will, not being evil according to their nature, not having been engraved with ignorance, not happening to be night and darkness according to essence, but having become evil by habit and pursuits in the attempt of such things, let us examine this reasoning.

Nature, on the one hand, is blind (and that not in the least) and will become scanty in sight, and ignorance itself will gain not one drop of knowledge on its own, and night itself and the darkness it has thus produced will not be transformed into a glimmer of light. On the other hand, the demons reveal that they knew the Saviour and Lord, saying together: "We know who you are", saying: "The Son of the living God".[43] Yet ignorance cannot know and a blind nature cannot see. They knew and, having known, they speak the truth and speak without calumny. For they say the truth, even though not with an honourable disposition. They are no longer accused of a "blind nature" or "ignorance". For truly they would not see in the least nor would they be supplicant, nor would they have submitted to the thing being said, nor would they have discerned what was revealed, but they would have supposed that he was not different from them, and the same as them.

For behold, reasonless beings are between prudence and imprudence, being unable to know what are prudent decisions and what are imprudent decisions. If the demons knew and, having known decision, set themselves free from

---

[43] Mark 1:24.

indecision, having adjudicated in such a manner through a judicial decision, then in this it is proven that not nature but free will is guiding. For free will, whether in a state of understanding or in a state of falling, nevertheless has not been released from being reasonable but maintains this (state) incorrupt.

Thus, even demons recognised him, beseeched him, and begged of him that he might not order them to go into the abyss. If they were children of the abyss, if they had a natural relationship to the abyss, why do they flee natural things? Why do they beg exemption from their own root cause? For they have greeted themselves, believing the natural relationship to be a respite. For among natural relations a recovery occurs, but among strangers, distress. Furthermore, it was necessary that they beg of Jesus; even more, that they demand exemption from this particular material world, where they, earnest and capable, welcome their arrival at the abyss. Instead they are those who demand exemption, guard themselves, and cannot bear to leave there. But begging for an indulgence from this invective, they have given sufficient sign that they did not have any natural relationship with the place of correction.

For never does something afflict itself but anything that is afflicted is afflicted by another. For it is necessary that affliction of oneself is not affliction, but another thing, engendered in order to suffer or to be afflicted. Look, fire does not burn itself, but another thing, and does not destroy itself. Look, water does not drown itself, for it knows how to drown other things but cannot drown itself. Look, air does not know how to blow against itself since every agent and afflicter afflicts and gives pain to another.

But if the abyss is evil and the demons are afflicted by the abyss, and the abyss is a torture-chamber, but the demons are tortured, they are no longer tortured by something of the same kind but, being other, they are tortured by another, no longer of this nature nor of its essence. For the abyss has been shown to be of another essence. And since the demons are of another kind and another essence than the abyss, what has been said is sufficient.

30

Besides, the same abyss is a torture-chamber and a place of correction, yet not everlasting and uncreated, but having been created at some later time, having been made sometime later as a cure and a remedy for those who have sinned. For holy are the scourges that are a cure for those who have sinned. Holy are the blows that are a remedy befalling those who have fallen. For the blows occur not in order that they might become evil, but rather, the scourgings occur in order that they might not become evil. For the evil ones who are distressed by the blows reduce their evil through the scourging. Because of this, we do not complain of the abyss but rather know that it has been created to be a torture-chamber and a place of correction, that is, a means of teaching self-control to those who have sinned.

If the abyss is a torture-chamber and a torture device but the demons are wrenched and tortured and have a nature susceptible to torture and are even capable of having a sense of pain, are subject to the punishment, and have a perception of the corrections, how are they unoriginate beings? How are they eternal? How did they not begin at some time? How are they not dispassionate in themselves, able to suffer and able to be punished?

For never will something unoriginate suffer anything or be punished by something but, having a beginning from itself, it remains in itself. Not having received its origin from another, it does not receive punishment from another. Not claiming a cause, it will not claim the corrective punishment. Not having a beginning from another, it will not be judged by another. It will fear no one, since it received its existence from no one.

For why should it fear if it has complete composition? Or if it has complete perfection? Or if it is complete in itself and is self-ordered? Things that can be subject to suffering have a harmony that fears what can alter harmonies. What is able to suffer fears the agent.

If demons fear and are able to suffer, they are not unoriginate. For what is unoriginate is unaffected and unable to suffer, having its beginning outside the nature of originate things. Because they beseech Jesus, they exist through sensible perceptions and know what they are and know that they are able to suffer. For they were not ignorant of themselves. They did not consider themselves unaffected. The act of someone knowing himself and not being ignorant is a token and sign of sensible perception. But if they feared because they are susceptible, and beseeched Jesus while fearing and beseeched the one who is powerful, they were not ignorant of the one hunting them down. For their same plea testifies that they had known the one hunting them down. And because they were susceptible and were sufferers, they were not ignorant that the one hunting them down was the Lord and king of all things, showing through their plea that they are imposed upon.

We have provided these matters concerning the demons in order that the rationale concerning the demons might in no way lie idle. For it is possible to add to these things that, within itself, nature is all the same and has no difference within itself. For consider fire, which is completely the same within itself. Heat is not weaker somewhere within itself nor stronger somewhere within itself. It does not have something stronger or weaker. For with respect to natures, that which is stronger and that which is weaker are nothing. Where there is greater and weaker, there is no longer nature, but the free gift of free will. If it is written, even concerning demons, that: "He goes and brings seven other spirits more evil than himself",[44] and the gift is revealed from the word because there is on the one hand something evil, but on the other hand there

---

[44] Luke 11:26 and Matt 12:45.

is something more evil, a difference in evil, where, then, is "nature", being that it is not the same within itself, because one finds a difference in evil and the difference testifies on behalf of free will and not nature?

31
Enough of such arguments! Rather, let us argue against their myth-making by indicating the most important. Let us provide the necessary argument through words of refutation. "Evil", they say:

> was and was unoriginate. Yet God was and God is good and their places of residence were separated, each one getting free of the other with respect to itself. God marked off the boundaries of evil, but the ruler of evil marked off the boundaries of God and each one was by himself, and each one began on his own and managed what he had produced: the evil one in an evil manner and the good one in a good manner. The evil one is harming and violating his own things and is not removing his own things from the damage, but the good one is eternally good and helps and helps his own things and never refuses to help. For all helpful things have been produced from good.

Thus, they should explain these things: if evil was essential and was by itself, why the interruption? Why the separation so that the essences should not be commingled?

For if neither one built a wall, everything was mixed, and evil and virtue were the same; and both essences were poured out and kneaded together and the one was no longer separated from the other. Rather, the act of producing this inferior mixing did not help evil but harmed the good. And evil acted eternally but the good was damaged.

And what else did the good become except bound since it is unable to act by being eternally taken by evil and not doing its own things? For if it did not help its own cause and was unable to defend its own interests, but was weak with respect to its own cause, how could nature be good if it does not save its own cause and if it is unable to help a cause belonging to another?

For inasmuch as it existed as a good nature, it ought to have preserved its own matters unharmed and helped matters belonging to another. If it had wished to do neither of these (since it neither changed shameful matters nor has it preserved its own) but matters were despoiled and matters became worse, therefore harming itself and sanctioning against itself, how is it not violence and slander against the good?

How is the explanation itself not an advocacy for the Devil and a slander against God? Look, therefore, the Manichaeans have appeared as advocates on the Devil's behalf and as slanderers of God by disparaging and diminishing the prominence of God and exaggerating the powers of the Devil. For if that one always harmed from all eternity and never did not harm, but harmed the good things and passed by nothing, being helped by the good, and from all eternity acting unjustly and harming the good, how will he not appear great and mighty? But he will be shown to be powerless and nothing.

If, then, he was thus, what is that which builds the wall and divides? And was the wall in the middle between the essences in order that each one might not lay a hand upon the other essence, since some unnamed power lay between? One must ask whether the wall was made previously and by whom it was made. For if it was made and we say it was made from evil, the evil was, consequently, suspicious. And living in fear, so that it might not suffer, it sought security for itself by means of the wall. So, living in fear lest it suffer, it accomplished this and fled as a thief.

And when did it become suspicious? For if something has been negotiated, what kind of first war between matter and God do they mythologise in order that, being fearful, matter used a wall (living in fear lest it be overtaken)? But if it anticipated the combat and, not joining in a war, planned the wall, they declare a praise of it as a most cautious thing, displaying its caution and wisdom and unbinding their definition of matter, no longer considering it unwise and ignorant, but considering it most cautious and wise.

32

If, however, they say God acted and designed the wall, they are contriving two false accusations against God (both cowardice and an inability to command). They will be put to shame. For while caring for the wall, he had thrust it forward, being fearful and having recognised weakness in himself. For those who are always able to suffer think beforehand about a safeguard. Otherwise, he has not furnished the wall as a necessary precaution and one unable to be shaken (in which case the Satanic nature would not have snatched away a portion of the light).

However, if they say each is a self-originator, then from their reasoning some other third entity has been produced as an unoriginate entity. Was it either previously a third entity by means of essence or a third entity by means of quality (not having been formed as a copy of another entity but being some other entity next to another entity) so that it was not existing as God nor was it existing as Satan, but as some other thing next to God, some other thing next to Satan?

Of what sort would the third essence be, neither being good nor material nor being of both? For if they say that it is in the middle and neither good nor bad, they lie about this. For this middle and neutral entity will never exist by itself, but receives the representation of each and will come into being by means of participation in both, and has this state of being, being able to exist by means of participation in both.

Furthermore, there will no longer be an unbreakable and limiting wall, preventive of the attack of each. For being in the middle and changing form because of communion with one, it is inclined toward the one it has sought. Surely it would become divine if imitating the divine, or evil if stamped with evil. But if this occurred, then no longer is evil against virtue, but rather two advanced against one and this other one was besieged, being pressed hard by two. For where the inclination of the middle entity occurred, because the addition has occurred, that principle, revealed as double, performs the attack against the other.

If, however, they no longer say a wall exists in the middle and is dividing the essences bordering and drawing near to themselves, but rather an empty and open thing exists in the middle, culpable for the separation, they will again say what they do not know. For what is open and what is empty, or the conception of something empty and open? For if it is something, it is neither empty nor open. However, if it is nothing and is empty on account of this (because it is nothing) and on account of this is open (because it subsists as complete nothingness), how could non-entities divide entities? How does what does not exist at all separate whats subsists and exists? For the entities that do not at all exist will not be able to separate entities subsisting and existing. Such a refutation has been conveyed.

33

Yet because they still bring forth most deceitful and erroneous words, increasing in error and deceit, let us not remain silent. For they say: "The evil that is advancing and moving forward by itself injured itself and mistreated itself and, as it stood against the land of truth, it was horrified. It marvelled at the unexpected light. It forgot its own strife, it turned on what had been revealed, seized light, and absorbed what it beheld".[45]

Henceforth, in the future there will be much laughter and great mockery. At that time, every pagan myth will be trod upon, being conquered in this manner. For myths are told as myths and are believed in as myths. If this was told as a myth, was believed in as a myth, it would cause little damage, it conquers myths, and among the senseless, it is believed as truth!

For if as they[46] are declaring, evil, as one enraged, as one blockading itself on its own, as one who had extended its own borders, that it beheld light and was panic-stricken and ended its own battle and turned on what had been revealed and seized what it beheld, how will their words not appear powerless

---

[45] Sarapion might be quoting from a source or simply paraphrasing something he had heard or read. This quote seems to be a discussion of the Manichaean mythology, as noted in the introduction.

[46] Literally, "as you are declaring" (ὡς φατέ).

and deceiving?

For how did evil harm itself, destroy itself, obliterate itself, at one time consuming and at another time producing, if it was unoriginate? For it was destroyed by annulling itself and was no longer able to exist by utterly destroying itself! For if a part of itself has entities that are being utterly destroyed, what sort of security would be sufficient so that the whole is destroyed, since the natural parts are destroyed?

If, however, it both engendered itself and began to exist, and by beginning to exist from itself was also a begetter, how is it still an unoriginate thing? Therefore, they will no longer receive the refutation of their absurd teaching from another but from their own nonsense. For they utter many things, while contradicting themselves by uttering and they no longer wait to be embarrassed by another but, talking nonsense, they suffer this because of their own indiscretion. For how could something that can be destroyed, both admitting of dissolution and being able to be utterly destroyed, be unoriginate? How could it be that being is from itself? How did it not begin from another, from something so indestructible and incapable of suffering, since something able to be obliterated and utterly destroyed does not have its being from itself?

But if it is destroyed, as they[47] say (for this determines their[48] rationale, confessing that what is absorbed is a capture and the absorption of what had been absorbed is a destruction) and it is conquered and dissolved and is being destroyed and consumed, it will no longer give substance to the things that are disappearing. And by not having a secure and indestructible nature, it will no longer be assumed to be unoriginate. And by not existing as unoriginate, evil will appear neither beginningless nor endless, at one time not existing, but now seeming to buzz on alone. For what it is is not an essence but some sickness that had joined to the essence, being able to be separated from essences and *hypostases*.

That the Deceiver himself is who he is because of a fall and he fell because of a misstep, giving evidence of the fall and misstep by the removal of good characteristics, the prophet Isaiah testifies: "How the morning star that rose early has fallen from heaven",[49] since he had known the aforementioned, banished condition befalling the previous divine, radiant, and most holy condition. The Saviour also testifies in the Gospel, saying: "Behold! I see Satan falling as a flash of lightning from heaven".[50]

If, however, he was thus, and was so naturally, it would not on the one hand, somehow be called a fall and on the other, in some way a banishment. For what falls, falls from stasis and what is banished departs from some

---

[47] Literally, "as you say" (ὡς φατέ).
[48] Literally, "your" (ὑμέτερος).
[49] Isa 14:12.
[50] Luke 10:18.

abundance. If he is said to be in a condition of having fallen, then at one time he was in a condition of stasis and stability. Besides, if he is denounced as being among those who have fallen, he was not a poor man, nor was he ever a beggar since he has much abundance and he is judged to be among those who had fallen because of some sickness—a negation of the permanent abundance. Certainly, Scripture confesses the abundance when it says: "how the morning star has fallen". The name was abundance, and being "morning star", he had the actuality of the Morning Star besides its potentiality and abundance and possession, and having fallen from this, he became empty of it. He is poor in respect to the abundance of the "Morning Star" and roams about and is in dire peril, being both a beggar and a fallen being, the one previously having much abundance.

If, according to the Gospel, he is among those who fall and lie on the ground and, furthermore, are wallowing in the mud, he formerly stood and was able to say: "our feet were those that stood in your courts, O Jerusalem",[51] was able to hear: "stand firm, having girded your loins with truth",[52] and being able to hear this, he did not secure himself with the oracle that had been stated: "the one who thinks he is standing must watch lest he fall".[53]

And, having procured no form of security against such a thing, he wallows among such places to this day. For that which is always lying on the ground would not fall (for it lies on the ground). What is fallen and came to the ground will not come to fall out of what is firmly grounded and stands. What was always in need and never apprehended any abundance will never fall from such abundance. After all, it always has nothing and cannot fall, never having had anything. What has endured banishment and suffered happens to be away from much abundance and existence. Such is the first refutation.

34

But because, they say, evil, while further advancing and consuming itself and after being present to the light, robbed from the light and absorbed some of the light, it robs it of its dignity (which they have contrived on behalf of evil, against truth), let us not refuse to invalidate this. For with this argumentation, they exalt evil but denigrate truth, and they give resilience to evil but they propose a non-resilient truth. For if evil has robbed and the light has been robbed and, having a beginning, suffered and was something subject to suffering, according to them God is one who suffers while Satan is one who does not suffer, the one being able to suffer, the other being able to act. For since the light is a suffering being, he himself would be a suffering one, since he

---

[51] Ps 121:2 (122:2).
[52] Eph 6:14.
[53] 1 Cor 10:12.

is not other than the light. If God was able to suffer (and to suffer not because of himself but at the hands of the enemy and the one who struggles against him) and was able to give himself up, then he came into being inclined toward what is worse.

But how has the one who has a unified nature been separated from the things that are his own? For the things that are natural with respect to his nature have not been formed in order to be divided from themselves. If the light was unoriginate and was united to what is unoriginate, how has it ever been capable of being divided? How was it removed from itself and how did it become another thing contrary to itself? For if it served evil and, having been overpowered by evil, it henceforth preferred evil things and practiced evil things and did not know itself and no longer recognised itself, but had become forgetful of itself, and perceived itself to be such as it had become,[54] even an evil thing, their reasoning will be revealed as contradictory. For something unoriginate is neither ignorant of itself nor will it be another entity alongside itself, but it remains such as it was and it will never be removed from itself, never having a beginning in order to exist.

35

But because they utter old wives' tales and fables,[55] not knowing what they are saying, but being put to shame by their utterances, let us add the following in writing to our argument. If light could be changed and become another entity alongside itself and become inclined toward evil and forget itself and do precisely what evil does, then the rulers of evil were able to suffer this and to be changed into good instead. And since change prevails and alteration is mighty, how would it not rather be better to be changed from evil into virtue, than from good into evil?

How did God bear and allow the light to be overtaken? How has he not prevented the attack? How did he not guard his own things? How, after the abduction, did he not wish to procure the foreknowledge of those who were abducted? How, anticipating beforehand, does he not stop the attack? How, rather, has he not watched over invincible things? Otherwise, how has he not bestowed help upon the conquered and overtaken things? If he permitted this so that the light that has formed in the evil things might change the evil things (since the evil things are able to be changed), the "evil things" are no longer evil by nature, being capable of being changed and God receives as a "pledge" from the evil things the change contrary to their nature.

If God were convinced that it did not change and had not been naturally produced in order to be altered, how did he foolishly allow what is good

---

[54] Literally "as it is" (οἷόν ἐστι).
[55] 1 Tim 4:7.

to suffer damage but not to receive an advantage against what is evil? How is it that he knew these same evil things were not changed, yet he himself disregarded his own good things that were changed? For this premiss (that he is altered on account of the alteration of his own things that are of his own self, but matter is not being altered) is absurd!

36

This is the refutation of that line of argumentation so that we might shorten a longer instruction, being silent concerning their presentations: the battles, those invented fables, and the great battles, and so that what has been said about the beginning of the circumstances might be said as a starting point and a seed of investigations might begin. However, with respect to the Law, let us treat the matter fully (having sufficiently called into question their rationale concerning the beginning).

For they have made it their custom to accept the Gospel but have hurried to censure the Law and the Prophets, and they have misrepresented the entire ancient testimony, but they have presumed to honour the Gospels, while assuming the form of honour toward the Gospels instead, so that they might employ an assumed form as a bait for those who are being deceived. For it is not because they have agreed with the Gospels that they concede honour to the Gospels but because they have honoured the name of Jesus, faking the honour so that they might lay claim to those who are honouring, just as they wish.

For it was necessary for them, if they honoured the Gospels, not to cut up the Gospels, not to subtract a part of the Gospels, not to add a single thing, and not to add in writing to the Gospels their own teaching and opinion. Their tongues do not keep to these Gospels and they omit them when reading. At any rate, they have added (in writing) as much as they wished and subtracted the amount they have decided and, furthermore, they invoke the Gospel by name, not having preserved the corpus of the Gospel as a corpus, but they have made, according to their own desires, another corpus of Scriptures, even going so far as to take over the name "Gospel".

Indeed, they have dishonoured the Gospels more than the pagans! For while pagans do not accept the Gospels, even in not accepting them they do not utterly destroy them but only throw them off to the side, and they do not really trample upon the Scriptures. However, those who suppose themselves to have received the Gospels, trampled upon them, danced upon them, played tricks with the Scriptures, and have done the works of sorcerers and evil men. Those people did not believe. They have proclaimed themselves by means of open unbelief, and did not dare to study what they do not believe. These people, by intervening, have attempted to destroy the harmony and have ventured to destroy completely the symmetry by means of artificially devised teachings, having contrived the name "Gospel" as a prerequisite for their deceit.

For if they had known the Gospel, they would not have been ignorant of the Law. And if they failed to know the Law, how did they recognise Jesus? For without the Law, they do not receive Jesus. For the one longing for the completion thoroughly investigates the beginning, but the one who is a disdainer of the beginning is vainly impassioned, speaks empty things, and is unable to arrive at the goal. If "the fulfilment of the Law is Christ",[56] they labour in vain, being deserters of the Law, but proclaiming to know Jesus. If the Law does not speak, the Lord is not recognised. For the silence of the Law is ignorance of what is being proclaimed, but knowledge of the Lawgiver is full knowledge of what is declared beforehand.

If they listened to Moses, they would believe in the one who has appeared prior. Of course, the one who has resurrected himself is not believed in unless the Law creates faith in those who hear. For even a certain someone once said: "Send Lazarus so that he might report to my brothers so that they might not go on this torturous journey",[57] with Abraham responding: "They have Moses and the Prophets".[58] This same person said: "Unless someone should rise from the dead, they will not believe",[59] but Abraham will be heard: "If they did not listen to Moses and the Prophets, then even if someone should rise from the dead, they will not listen".[60] Imagine that! The summoning of the one who resurrects himself does not contradict the providence of the Law and the Prophets.

For being flanked by the Law and the Prophets, Jesus did not think it right to be revealed without their company and, while being able to be testified to by the Father, he did not disdain the company of the saints; but desiring to present a most precise faith to the eyes of the apostles, as he led them up on the mountain and was transfigured, he displayed Moses and Elijah in order that the company of their great holiness might become a testimony and so that whoever receives Jesus might not disdain those associated with him, so that one might not be dishonouring him or his kingdom by disparaging those who flank him and his servants.

At any rate, the Saviour has satisfied such a concern regarding the Law and the Prophets, since he in no way left anything in the Law unfulfilled, but effected everything that is written, he cries: "I came not to destroy the Law, but to fulfil it".[61] And he goes into the temple and throws out the disgusting treasuries so that having restored a pure house, he might present (through this act) a most precise faith, since he is the one who manages both his own and his

---

[56] Rom 10:4.
[57] Luke 16:24, 27-28. Sarapion's citation appears to be a conflation.
[58] Luke 16:29.
[59] Luke 16:30.
[60] Luke 16:31.
[61] Matt 5:17.

Father's affairs. For he cries: "The house of my Father shall be called a house of payer, but you have made it a den of thieves".[62]

Because the oracles that can put to shame their wicked teaching are numberless, we (so that we might not draw the argument out at length, by using more words) should entrust others to use corresponding arguments from what has been said. We, having suitably furnished what is necessary against the very things antithetical to the oracles, shall continue.

37

They receive the Gospel but do not receive the Law. For they do not receive the entire Holy Gospel. For they would have received the Law if they had received the entire Gospel. But now, having first corrupted the Gospel, they obviously do not receive the Law. Therefore, they are refuted on account of having pirated the Gospel while not being sustained by the Law. If they testify to the Gospel and do not honour the Law, they have dishonoured their testimony! For it is no longer dishonour against the Law but want of faith in their testimony.

Besides, if one of the Gospels testified to something but another was silent, and the dishonour came to be against one only, the other Gospels would not be silent, regarding the dishonour against the one to be a general dishonour against them all. If Mark says: "The beginning of the Gospel of Jesus Christ, just as it is written in the Prophet Isaiah",[63] and Matthew: "A book concerning the origin of Jesus Christ, Son of David, Son of Abraham",[64] and he has known Abraham as the forefather of the begetting according to the flesh and honours David, and he unites the Gospel with the Law and has perceived the Law as the origin of the Gospel, the Saviour speaks the truth by saying: "The one who rejects you, rejects me".[65] For the dishonour no longer stands just against the Law, but rises up against the Saviour himself.

Let the Jews also hear: "If you would have listened to Moses, you would have listened to me, for that man wrote concerning me".[66] Let the Manichaeans also listen: if you have heard the Gospel, you would have heard the Law. For the Gospel has been written because of the Law! But Jews, taking a veil,[67] have neither understood the Law nor recognised the one who has been proclaimed. The heretics "possess eyes that do not see and possess ears that do not hear",[68]

---

[62] Matt 21:13. See also Mark 11:17 and Luke 19:46.
[63] Mark 1:1.
[64] Matt 1:1.
[65] Luke 10:16.
[66] John 5:46.
[67] See 2 Cor 3:12-4:6, where St Paul contrasts the scriptural reading of the Christians with that of the Jews, who wear a veil to that present day in the synagogues and do not realise that the veil is removed only by reading the Scriptures in the light of Christ.
[68] Jer 5:21.

and because they have not looked into the Gospels, they fight against the Law. For look, John cries: "there came a man, sent from God, whose name was John. This man came as a witness in order that he might testify concerning the Light".[69] Jesus knows the witness, he knows what is testified to, and he announces the witness by saying: "The Law and the Prophets were until John came".[70] Therefore, John testifies and the Law is a witness. Also, if the Law is a witness and the Law is called to witness, look how great an absurdity unbelief practises in the case of witnesses!

And concerning these things that have been uttered, Luke also is not silent about such things. For he declares the same message and utters in harmony with the others and fully describes how just after Gabriel appeared to Mary, he gave a heavenly greeting, saying: "Hail! Most highly favoured one! The Lord is with you!"[71] But since that lady was perplexed by the saying, she also pondered within herself, saying: "What sort of greeting might this be?"[72] Gabriel said: "Do not fear, Mary, for you have found favour before the face of God and behold! You shall conceive in your womb and shall bear a son and you will call his name Jesus. He will be great and will be called Son of the Most High and the Lord will give to him the throne of his father David and he will rule into the ages, and of his kingdom there will be no end".[73] So David is honoured and is confessed to be a father of the Saviour and the sovereignty remains and is handed over to the Lord and it does not receive an end, the sovereignty being exalted by the one who is without end.

38

Besides, these are the beginnings of the Gospels. For it was necessary for us to construct the argument from the beginnings in order that someone, slowly proceeding from here through the argument in this way, might perceive both the coherence and the harmony of the stories of all the Gospels. Since, however, the apostolic ministry preserves the Gospel character and Paul knows this and he measures his own service of sufferings as an allotment of the Gospel (for he says: "According to my Gospel in Jesus Christ"[74]), let us not leave aside the beginnings of the Apostle, but let us come to them through a recollection, so that having arrived at all his writings and the beginnings of the writings, we might treat the Law with concord.

So, writing to the Hebrews, he says: "Formerly, God spoke in diverse and various ways through the prophets, but in these last days, he spoke to us

---

[69] John 1:6-7a.
[70] Luke 16:16.
[71] Luke 1:28.
[72] Luke 1:29.
[73] Luke 1:30-33.
[74] Rom 2:16.

through his Son, whom he appointed an heir of all things, through whom he also made all the ages".[75] Here, he knows the Father of the Son and, knowing about the Father of the Son, he does not divide the matter, is not silent concerning the ancient things, and does not attribute them to other prophets but to the God of the prophets and the Father of the Son. Paul has neither divided nor cleaved in two, but proclaims a complete message about the one who has been worshipped by those prophets and who has produced this one. On the one hand, the Father is the begetter of this one while, on the other hand, he makes use of these prophets as worshippers and supplicants. For the prophets are supplicants of his and the Son of this Father is the Christ.

If you honour the Son but speak slanderously against the supplicants and revile them, you utter what you wish through your mouth. Do you see that the Son is irritated? He does not tolerate the Father being mistreated. For if the Father has reckoned the dishonour of the Son as his own dishonour, how much more will the Son consider the mistreatment of the Father as his own belittlement?[76]

39

In order that we might move forward a little and so that we might shame them a little, let us attack their position in this way: if the Law is from God, why do they not receive the Law? If you speak slanderously against the Law, whose words and voice are the Law? Through whose power have the things written of the Law been spoken?

For here the heretics separate themselves and no longer reason similarly, but contradict themselves. So it is with the Valentinians and so it is with the Manichaeans, though Marcionites testify spittle and not words against the Law. So the Valentinians say the God of the Law was one who is righteous and, being one righteous, he was not the Father of the Son. Jesus, they say, is good and the Father is good and so the Father of the Son is good and what is begotten is good, but the God of the Law is righteous.

And so, reasoning such things, they have not considered what sort of relation a just object has toward what is good, and that if something is just, it is also good, and if something is good, it is also just. They have not conceived of this in their imagination. And not being able to possess such imaginations, let them be questioned concerning this alone: if the God of the Law is just and he is not the Father of the Son, Jesus is not just.

How do we demand justice from the Son? If he has not been begotten by the just one, how does he judge? How does he decree judgment? How has he

---

[75] Heb 1:1-2.
[76] 1 John 2:22-23.

been entrusted with the judgment seat by the Father? How does he repay each person according to what he/she has done?[77] How does Paul tell the truth, saying: "God contributes to the good for those who, through endurance in good works, seek after everlasting life, but for those who are misled by injustice because of selfish ambition, wrath and indignation and affliction and distress upon the entire soul of the man who accomplishes evil"?[78] For the words are meaningless if the premiss of justice, with respect to the Son, is not conceded.

But if the punishment against those who have fallen is established and the authority of the just one produces the amount of the punishment, but honours and gifts are stored up for those who are of good repute, and honour is weighed by the discrimination of the just one, how are they not put asunder and humbled because of their indiscretion? If the Only-begotten is such a just one but the Father is not such a just one, likeness is no longer begotten from likeness, no longer the image[79] of the Begetter, no longer the "stamped image",[80] no longer the "radiance".[81] No longer would it be that "he who sees the Son sees the Father"[82] if the Son did not possess all that the Father possesses. And yet the Saviour cries out in the Gospel: "O just Father, the world does not know you, but I know you".[83]

40

What shall we do? Turn our backs on the words of the Saviour? Shall we be faithless to what has been written or marvel at the word (since it is a word of truth), shall we determine that the Valentinians are like madmen[84] and the demon possessed, beyond the bounds of those worthy of God and holy gatherings?

But since we are permitting some absurdity by lengthening our argument against the heretics, and this problem is not dragging us about, let us invoke an argument and proceed against the underlying problem, after having carefully examined these things on account of their usefulness in order that this argument, kept completely silent, might not be taken for granted by us.

For evil has spoken against the Law in three separate ways and, having

---

[77] Rom 2:6. Neither Casey nor Fitschen cites this verse, but it seems to me very likely that it lies behind this question and is probably why Sarapion goes on to quote from the following verse.
[78] See Rom 2:7-9. See also Rom 8:28.
[79] Col 1:15.
[80] Heb 1:3.
[81] Ibid.
[82] John 14:9.
[83] John 17:25.
[84] See section three, where Sarapion refers to the "mania" of the Manichaeans, a clear pun on the name Mani. Sarapion here links the Valentinians to the "madmen" of his contemporary setting, the Manichaeans.

been useful to that same number of heretical divisions, it has served that same number of both servants and champions of blasphemy, having overtaken those willing to serve it, and so, through Valentinus, it belittled the Law and separated the Gospel from it and through Marcion the writing of the Law is some sort of miscarriage and through Mani it is something evil, without light, and of complete darkness.

For it accomplishes things like this. It contrives proclamations like this. It speaks empty things through a composition of proclamations astounding undisciplined ears. On account of such matters, it is necessary to ask: if that evil wrote the Law, that one without light, being complete darkness through and through, did it know the advent of Jesus? Did it know his arrival? How, when the circumstances had not yet occurred, did it perceive what God determined and declared and revealed beforehand? For from the beginning, the writings of the Law clearly testify to the arrival of the Son.

However, if they say the Law did not reveal and the Prophets did not proclaim, they who utter against what was foreseen will be refuted. Whereby we are not devising their refutation, but the Gospels themselves are publicly speaking against them, here and there, by crying out somewhere: "so that what was spoken through Isaiah the prophet might be fulfilled;"[85] and somewhere: "I came not to destroy the Law, but to fulfil it".[86] Now, if those who are clearly being refuted by this agree, what do they answer? For if "no one knows the things of God except the Spirit of God",[87] and the one writing the Law knew the things of God and knew as much as God determined and, on account of this, has written from observation and understanding, the one writing, then, was from God and was God and was in God and, on account of this, God has spoken however much he determined, since he is the one knowing things of God and is not ignorant.

If no one knows our heart, but only the Creator knows and our heart escapes the notice of others, though is unable to escape God's notice, but what God determined, evil was not ignorant of, but knew, and this one determined but that one knew, how do they not give to evil greater greatness, since it is able to understand the hidden will of God? How do they not slanderously say God is unable to shield himself from evil? Besides, we should laugh at the men who, when they are doing something against their opponents, make their scheme easy to detect. Those devising such an argument do not see that they bring about laughter against God because the God who leads the battle against evil has not protected his own hidden schemes but allowed these very things to become easy to detect for evil. If the divine and angelic powers are unable

---

[85] Matt 4:14. See also 12:17.
[86] Matt 5:17.
[87] 1 Cor 2:11.

to know what the Father determines, the Son only knowing and exegeting (since "no one has ever seen God; the Only-Begotten Son, the one who is in the bosom of the Father, that one has exegeted"[88]), how did the evil powers know the things of God, since the divine powers themselves were unable to know these things, unless a bequeathing of knowledge were transmitted from the exegesis of the Only-Begotten one?

However, because the Law itself, in anticipation, describes in full all things concerning his coming ("behold, the Virgin carries a child in her womb and will bear a Son"[89]), one prophet knows the place ("and you, Bethlehem, land of Judah, are by no means least amongst the rulers of Judah"[90]), another one the location of the setting ("the ox knows its Master and the donkey his Lord's crib"[91]) **and another the flight into** Egypt and the return from Egypt ("from Egypt have I called my Son"[92]), and another the home that was his in his youth ("land of Zebulon, land of Naphtali, on the road by the sea, across the Jordan: the people sitting in darkness have seen a great light"[93]) and another is not ignorant of the forerunner ("a voice of one crying in the desert: prepare the way of the Lord, make his paths straight").[94]

In short, if someone gathering up the prophesies from the Law would wish to bring together the entire Gospel, in this way writing down the things that have been effected through prophetic words, he will reveal himself to be someone fond of learning and studious of words, one who exegetes (not apart from the Spirit) his instructions, his teachings, his baptism, the fulfilment of signs, the judgment that came to pass, the betrayal by Judas, the plan of salvation on the erect scaffolding, the gall and vinegar given to him in his thirst, the burial itself, and the tomb, the transaction in Hades, the Resurrection itself, and, finally, the Ascension. Then, henceforth, he will also cry: "Lift up the gates you rulers, and be lifted up, everlasting gates, and the king of glory will come in".[95] And then this one will also add what has been written by **David**: "The Lord said to my Lord, 'Sit at my right hand until I make your enemies your footstool.'"[96]

Therefore, if the Law accurately described the coming of the Son and transmitted this long ago, the law is no longer discredited and is no longer attributed to another. The one who has begotten has announced beforehand.

---

[88] John 1:18.
[89] Isa 7:14.
[90] Mic 5:2, according to Matt 2:6.
[91] Isa 1:3.
[92] Hos 11:1, according to Matt 2:15.
[93] Isa 9:2, according to Matt 4:15-16.
[94] Isa 40:3, according to Matt 3:3.
[95] Ps 23:7 (24:7).
[96] Ps 109:1 (110:1).

The one who determined through his Word preconceived the circumstances. God has begotten. God says: "You are my Son; today I have begotten you".[97] God dispatched. God spoke through Moses: "The Lord God will raise up a prophet for you from amongst your brethren. You will listen to him even so far as everything he may say to you".[98] God determined and, while determining, he did not keep silent. He indicated his will beforehand, producing faith through the things he indicated beforehand. He says: "For his name is called messenger of great counsel, wonderful, counselor, ruler of peace, Father of the ages to come".[99]

41
Such is the refutation of these things. Because they attribute the Law to evil, what do they say when some one of them will inquire whether an evil man exhorts evil things and is not able not to exhort evil things or if at some point he will exhort and counsel good things? For if they say that someone is naturally disposed to exhort fine things or to counsel good things, they refute their own position again. For the one who is not exhorting evil things is no longer evil and the one who is counselling good things is no longer evil.

Besides, if a good choice in no way comes forth from an evil man, from what sort of category do they say these exhortations are: "Do not fornicate, do not commit adultery, do not steal, do not bear false witness"?[100] From what sort of category do they say is this written exhortation: "Do not make an idol for yourself nor any likeness: neither of whatever is in the sky nor whatever is on the earth nor whatever is in the waters"?[101] From what class will they say these matters of importance are: "Do not covet your brother's ox or his donkey or his wife or any of his cattle"?[102] For if they will say such things are holy, divine, and lovely, they will be shamed by the exhortations since they have not perceived the greatness of the one who has counselled. But if they say these are evil things and discredited, and it is evil not to fornicate and it is evil not to covet property of others and such are the evil things, look at what sort of things they will consider good things! Observe that they are panderers of desires and patrons of idols and inventors of shameful covetousness.

For by slandering the Law, they serve as ambassadors of lawlessness! Those who ostracise and get rid of the Law, which destroys desires, abolishes deceit and hinders superstition, what else do they do than bring into the house malicious desires and introduce covetousness? In order that a desire may enter

---
[97] Ps 2:7.
[98] Deut 18:15-16a.
[99] Isa 9:6.
[100] Exod 20:13-16.
[101] Exod 20:4.
[102] Exod 20:17.

unrestrained into their thoughts, they expelled the Law from their homes so that by not using the Law they might be turned against the Law, but also that they might present their ears as having been sold out to covetousness (by somehow shaking off the Law).

The Law is revealed to be a destroyer of evil but they attempted, ignorantly and rudely, to slander the Law. The Law hates evil, but they hate the Law. The Law abolishes superstition but they dare to destroy the Law.

42

Therefore let us compare the matters of importance. If the Law stands against evil but they fight against the Law, they are angered for the sake of evil, because the Law reproaches evil. For by not bearing the reproach of evil, they have slandered the Law. In order that the reproach against evil might not prevail, the Law has been slandered.

If the Law destroys idols and abolishes polytheism, but they have employed weapons against the Law, they have clearly proclaimed polytheism. For in order that the teaching of polytheism might prevail, the instruction of the Law (that which says: "Hear, O Israel! The Lord your God is one",[103] and "Love the Lord your God",[104] and "Do not, having looked up to the sky and having seen the sun and the moon, worship them"[105]) has been hindered by them. Against these words they have employed weapons. Against these instructions they sharpened the tongue, making it rough like a knife.

Because of this, they are under the influence of demons and reverence all things, and know nothing except to worship everything, and they always fall on the ground and they do not have an enlightened mind and they wander about and roam about in their thoughts. They have made everything into gods with authority, and they have held fast to error. They have vanquished the pagans, having become more pagan than the pagans, in numbers and vanity and by dulling their own ignorance through their great absurdity.

43

Now, so that someone who uses a most deceptive cunning may not deliberately say: "The Law demeaned itself and, after carrying off some of the good it presented them as its own, desiring to exalt its own absurdities, and interspersed portions of the good things, having made haste to conceal the other things with the good portions", come, let us first repeat: that nothing absurd can be revealed from the Law, and let this produce the refutation of their absurdity. Second, if after proceeding against evil it repelled some portion of evil, having

---

[103] Deut 6:4.
[104] Deut 6:5.
[105] Deut 4:19.

set free from every portion of evil through their act of believing, then no longer can the Law be revealed as demeaning itself, but as an enemy and opponent of evil. Third, if evil surrounded some of the good things and did not associate every form of virtue with the Scriptures, so that, if some virtuous things were revealed as having been written while greater things have been omitted, their refutation would have some force. However, if entirely all of the good things have been included in the writings of the Law, let us marvel at the Law and confess the Law of God and call it the instruction of the Father, and let us add: they are the ones who have possessed a deceitful and debased mind.

Therefore, because the Law contains not one portion of evil interspersed within it and, having obstructed every portion of evil, does not draw back from any other, but the Law is pure and holy and the Law of God, Paul cries: "Therefore, the Law is holy and the commandment holy, righteous, and good. For we know that the Law is spiritual".[106] For what is holy and spiritual and good is free from every absurdity and is in no way entangled in culpability. It is exalted with virtues and speaks for God. For the instruction on behalf of God is not elicited from another arrangement, but is composed through the authority of the Spirit. "For God is Spirit and those who worship him must worship in spirit and truth."[107] The Law, being spiritual, provides instruction on behalf of God and is able to accuse other things, and is itself interrogated by no one.[108] By how much more is the spiritual Law itself able to interrogate the arguments, than others, while it will not be interrogated itself by anyone?

44

Because the Law destroyed every form of evil and did not overlook one portion, but proceeded against every form of evil, restraining and destroying it, it is clear from the conditions concerning evil that there are four forms of evil: imprudence, intemperance, cowardice, and injustice. If the Law were to have concealed something bad, the Law would be imperfect.[109] But if it proceeded against evil and caused evil's destruction, destroying (in advance) every form of evil, evil is clearly reduced by the Law, not having been allowed to retain even a remnant.

At any rate, wherever the Law prevails and provides resiliency to obedience, not one drop of evil is found. But wherever it is relaxed, evil goes about despoiling and overrunning, proceeding on its own authority, having acquired authority over the soul in one who is unguarded. For the Law cries:

---

[106] Rom 7:12, 14a.
[107] John 4:24.
[108] 2 Cor 2:15.

[109] There is a possible double meaning, here, as Sarapion says the Law would be without a *telos*, which he has earlier informed the reader is Jesus the Christ. In other words, if the Law has concealed something, then Christ is not its *telos*.

"If my people had listened to me, if Israel had walked in my ways, I would have very quickly put down their enemies".[110] For when the Law persuades, evil becomes weak, lying on the ground and unable to resist the soul. For if: "Your Law is a lamp to my feet and a light to my paths",[111] every stumbling has been done away with, since the heart has been found illumined and radiant. For even if that one is young and might be at an age at which it is easy to slip, but should keep guard over his words, persevering unerringly, he will cry: "In what manner will a young man make his way? By guarding your words".[112] Having procured the power of never falling, concealing deep within himself, in his thoughts, the teachings of the Law, he says: "In my heart I treasured your oracles, so that I would not sin against you".[113]

In this way, having set up the Law as guard and sentry, he will perceive how the Law expels each of the forms of evil, expelling imprudence by saying what is written: "Do not become like a horse or mule, which are not perceptive";[114] banishing cowardice through the speaking oracle: "Do not fear when a man becomes rich. Do not fear the reproach of men and do not be overcome by their contempt".[115] Fear God and you will be strong. Do not fear another besides him. For having shaken off cowardice there, the Law, having both inspired confidence and instilled courage, cries: "The righteous one has prevailed like a lion, which neither fears nor falls down in fear before a beast".[116] And having destroyed two forms of evil, imprudence and cowardice, it also destroys intemperance at the same time, saying: "Do not fornicate. Do not commit adultery".[117] Wherever the passions are curtailed, the rein of self-control is found in the mind. And having simultaneously destroyed three forms of evil, it also destroys injustice: "Do not make for yourselves large and small standards. Just and equal standards shall exist among you".[118] So having done away with all the types of evil together, and every form of evil having been abolished, evil is destroyed, no longer being able to haunt the mind.

---

[110] Ps 80:14 (81:13-14).
[111] Ps 118:105 (119:105).
[112] Ps 118:9 (119:9).
[113] Ps 118:11 (119:11).
[114] Ps 31:9 (32:9).
[115] Ps 48:17 (49:16) and Isa 51:7. Casey continues the quotation into the next two sentences. However, he gives only the reference to Ps 48:17 (49:16). Fitschen includes only two sentences in quotations, referring to Ps 48:17 for the first sentence and Isa 51:7 for the second. I have not found clear biblical references for the second two sentences, such that I am inclined to agree with the way Fitschen has handled this scriptural reference by Sarapion.
[116] Prov 28:1 and 30:30.
[117] Exod 20:13.
[118] Lev 19:35-36.

45

Therefore what sort of form of absurdity has the Law not abolished? What portion of pleasure has it not destroyed? Which cowardice? What kinds of imprudence? Did it not proceed against so much, abolishing desire, so as to manage the eyes, and not to spare the ears and not to neglect the tongue? "For I made a covenant with my eyes and I will not take notice of a young virgin."[119] The one who is holy first manages the eyes so that desire, by exciting the soul, might not lead it into a snare of desire. One of the holy ones cried: "Do not covet the beauty of another",[120] so that malicious desire might not receive the hope of entering by seizing the entrance gates to the soul but, having been expelled from the gates, might possess a hopeless plan. Extending also to the ears and tongue, the Law placed guards and sentries for the members, not conceding its own position, but cried: "Set, O Lord, a guard over my mouth and a gate of fortification around my lips",[121] so that an absurd argument (apart from what is beneficial) coming forth as an incitement of malicious desire might not be effective for the one uttering shameful things. But also having charge over the loins (such that despite having been agitated here and there, the mind is not captive), the Law planned ahead, exhorting: "Thus you shall eat the Passover feast: your loins having been girded",[122] so that we might not attempt a reckless action (by having ungirded members), but might find, having been thus girded, the best order for our circumstances.

So the forms of desire having been destroyed in advance, the Law also proceeded against the forms of the mind and against the forms of injustice. For if the act of taking the possessions of another (and taking by force and against the other's will) is unjust, and taking the possessions of another (whether to give to others or to squander them wastefully) is a form of injustice, then the one hindering the honour of God is unjust, as is the one who is rendering God's honour to wooden idols and demons, both squandering the honour and being wasteful in one's mind. For the one who squanders thus wastefully what is his own is not as unjust as the one who removes the great abundance, the honour of God, from his mind. For in as much as the abundance of knowledge unites with the soul, the person's disposition is directed toward God. When, however, it has been completely subdued, exhausted, and become destitute, then it henceforth brings one's honour down to a wooden idol and a work of cunning. Because of this, the Apostle, having stood against unjust superstition, said: "Even greediness, anything which is idolatry".[123]

---

[119] Job 31:1.
[120] Sir 9:8.
[121] Ps 140:3 (141:3).
[122] Exod 12:11.
[123] Col 3:5.

46

Since, therefore, the most grievous aspect of injustice is ignorance toward God and the most insignificant is a sin against men, injustice is distinguished in two ways: one is the ignorance toward God and the other is the sin against men. The written Law ruled against both. First, it cries: "You shall not make idols for yourself of any likeness",[124] so that, by squandering the honour due to the Creator, you might not utterly destroy it all together. And he was naturally angry because of the people, when having made a calf, they cried: "These are your gods, Israel, which led you out of the land of Egypt".[125] For since they rendered the gifts of the benefactor to that which could not be moved, and it was a most grievous injustice to render the abundance of the benefactor, the Creator, to a work of art and an engraved figure, truth has been set in motion and the Law written.

So injustice has been hindered and the pupil was disciplined and so, the desire of injustice being destroyed in advance, the Law also destroyed the injustice against the human race. So, first, it has not wanted the love of wealth to be born in the soul, since the love of wealth brings forth injustices and the desire for money begets excesses. "For the root of evils is the love of money",[126] and injustices and excesses will be branches and twigs of the love of money. And since excess and injustice begin from the love of money, the Law anticipates this, destroys it in advance, and announces beforehand: "Whenever wealth might flow in, do not give your heart over to it",[127] so that one might not receive a ruined mind[128] by means of the flowing of wealth caused by the flood of wealth. For if wealth flows and is not stable, the mind naturally withstands this when it has not utterly destroyed its own stability by means of the flood of wealth.

Also since the love of money causes distress and the love of glory, pillaging the mind by means of what is new and exuberant...,[129] the Law also improvised this passion ("I saw the ungodly man lifting himself up and exalting himself like the cedars of Lebanon, and I went by and behold, he was no more")[130] so that the mind might not at all pawn the greatness of itself after being led astray by the flower of youth that easily dies away, but transcending these things it holds fast to the love of truth.

---

[124] Exod 20:4.
[125] Exod 32:4.
[126] 1 Tim 6:10.
[127] Ps 61:10 (62:10).
[128] Literally a mind that has flowed together (συρρέουσαν τὴν διάνοιαν).
[129] There is a lacuna within the text. I have left out τῆς δόξης, not knowing exactly how to place it within this sentence. Fitschen links it to "what is new and exuberant", speaking of "fame which is new and flowering". I believe this is forced, but have no alternative.
[130] Ps 36:35-36 (37:35–36).

So on account of this, the Law honours commensurability and expels injustice and provides divine habitations to those who have maintained commensurability, and thus cries: "Lord, who will sojourn in your tabernacle or who will dwell on your holy mountain? The one who walks blamelessly and works righteousness, speaking the truth with his heart",[131] so that having banished every form of the love of wealth, it might not allow a place for injustice.

Thus the Law by attacking has destroyed every form. On account of this, the one who proclaims according to the Law proclaims on behalf of the truth. On account of this, those who work for truth are not angry with the Law proclaiming against evil. Once the Saviour spoke against the love of wealth and the Jews were angry. For the love of wealth worked anger against the one speaking.[132]

Of course, when a teacher lectures a heedless child concerning heedlessness, he is hated by the one being taught. For everyone who eradicates the passion of the time of youth is hated because of the love of malicious pleasures. Because of this, the Law has been hated by the heretics. Since it advanced against the passions, proceeded against sins, and lectured to those loving such things, they could not bear its action.

47

In order that our arguments may yet become most magnificent and the absurdity of the heretics may be revealed as having unjustly proceeded against the Law, let us not put in writing, by way of argument, only that the Law destroys every form of evil, but let us state further, for instruction, that it also indicates and counsels every form of virtue. For if the Law destroyed all evils but did not insert all virtues, the Law fell short, omitting the training of virtues, since, having banished all evils, it is no longer pursuing all the virtues for the soul. However, when it might be revealed from argument that all the virtues are laid down with the Law and the Prophets, how is it not necessary to marvel and accept the Law of God?

For there exist four virtues: prudence, self-control, courage, and **righteousness. The virtues are entirely within the Law.** On account of this, the

---

[131] Ps 14:1–2 (15:1–2).

[132] While the exact biblical reference remains unclear to me, the cleansing of the temple seems to be the most likely. In **Mark 11 we learn that after this, the chief priests and scribes plotted to kill him and Matt 21 tells us that they became angry upon learning of it. There are other passages which could be intended, though they do not fit** Sarapion's description quite as well. Matt 19 presents a situation where the disciples are astounded at Jesus' statement concerning a rich man and a camel passing through a needle's eye. Likewise, Matt 13:22 and Luke 8:14 speak of wealth or riches choking out faith, and in Matt 6:24 Jesus says we cannot serve two masters, and at the end of his sayings, the crowd is astounded.

one who wills to be self-controlled has the Law's lessons. The one striving to be prudent, by taking his starting-points from the Law, will gain distinction in what he does. The one willing to be courageous, let him be anointed with precepts. Let the one striving toward righteousness hold fast in order to cleave to the standard of righteousness that he might not do an unjust thing, doing all things through the standard of righteousness. Let the one partaking of prudence through comprehension speak: "God taught me wisdom and the judgment of men is not in me",[133] in order that having forced out this imagined and misguided thing, he might welcome what is best and divine.

Whoever is perceptive when seeking will find innumerable examples of self-control, emulating the examples and receiving the many examples of self-control as an anointing. That young man[134] in his prime, delivered up by his brothers, and purchased by the Egyptians, exchanged the freedom of the body [for slavery], having maintained an unchangeable freedom of the soul by having been stripped of his garments in order that he might not strip off self-control, his clothes having been taken off by force while self-control was not torn away by force. He chose to suffer so that he might not fall into the passion of malicious pleasure. Having come into a state of captivity instead of passions of pleasure, he is the one who chose to be a prisoner so that he might not be found bound to pleasure. He is the one who preferred the malice of shameful actions. He is the one who was considered shameful and did not want to be shameful. For he reckoned it more beautiful to be considered shameful than to be shameful and get away with something. For by becoming shameful and concealing shame, he would have had to fear God as a witness, but being considered shameful, he was satisfied with having his master as a witness to the things that happened. This is an example of self-control and for courage there are many others.

Judith is a befitting example of courage.[135] She was a weak woman and was feeble and was cowardly, since she was a weak woman, but was also daring and courageous, since she was faithful. The things that were impossible in the expectations of men, she exhibited as possible through courage. She attributed unexpected events to faith and hope, having been strong in courageous faith. For the walls opened and the young woman came forth and came forth with only a handmaiden, not afraid of suspicion because of her beauty, not being wary of the swords, not fearing that he[136] might have sexual intercourse with her and that she might not survive the forced licentiousness, not fearing that she might suffer something unexpected by a sword, but, rather, conquering

---

[133] Prov 30:2.
[134] Sarapion refers to Joseph here, reflecting upon the portions of Joseph's story from chapters 37 and 39 of Genesis.
[135] See especially chapters 8-13 of Judith.
[136] The general, Holofernes.

the fear of the sword by courage and commending what is beautiful to God. For she believed God to be the trustworthy guard of beauty. She regarded swords as dry sticks, weaker than papyrus, having trod upon cowardice with a courageous disposition. The woman disregarded such fears yet was not judged as daring. Neither did she acquiesce to the charge of being crude. For the decisions that she made were not aimless, in which case she could have been accussed of being crude. The things that she willed, she carried out. The things she had carefully considered were brought to completion. She is marvelled at because of this, since she mixed prudence with courage and since as much as she planned, she brought to completion.

While receiving the example of this courage, we will receive one of righteousness when Abraham defended and fought for the one being treated unjustly.[137] After helping him, he heard from those who were rescued: "Take the horse and everything for yourself".[138] Hearing these things, he was not looking for financial gain, but was looking intently upon what is righteous and acknowledging that he received them as a gift and that in no way should one sell a gift, since charity is not put forth in order to be bought and sold. Those who take and sell gifts are unrighteous. Someone selling good deeds as items at a market does not act righteously. Let one sell a cloak and an heirloom in the markets, but, let the good deed, which is given as a gift through generosity of intention, to the one who needs it, remain unsold.

48

Therefore we have such an example of intention that it is not fitting for gifts and good deeds to be bought and sold for great wealth but the honour of each is protected so it is not ruined beforehand by the giving of wealth. So, by having related these things, we established that everything is laid down in the Law, both the destruction of evil and the accomplishment of virtue.

And since these are sufficient things for the purpose of humiliation and shame, we append something similar: for if there were the Gospels, then there was also the Law, but if the Law possesses nothing like the Gospel, the category would have been one of dissimilarity. But since the category is one of similarity, why do we tear apart similarity when tearing apart similarity is not self-sustaining?

The stamped image cries aloud of kinship.[139] The similarity indicates

---

[137] That is, Lot. See chapters 13 and 14 of Genesis.
[138] Gen 14:21. The rest of Sarapion's reflection is largely informed by verse 23, where Abraham declines to take what is offered lest he be made rich by the king of Sodom.
[139] Neither Casey nor Fitschen notes that χαραχτήρ, the subject of this sentence, seems almost certainly a reference to Heb 1:3, where St Paul uses this word in reference to Christ, calling him God's character, or impressed image. Given that verses 1 and 2 have Paul telling us that God spoke formerly through the prophets and lately through his Son, and Sarapion's

fellowship. They draw the mind to the one cause of all other things, the Father of the Saviour. The Law said: "Hear, O Israel, the Lord your God is one Lord".[140] The Gospel said: "No one is good except one, God".[141] Paul cried: "One God, from whom are all things".[142] And so, the Unbegotten one and the fatherless one has been perceived from the Law, the Saviour, and the Apostle.

Therefore, the begotten one is both begotten from the bosom and the Son of the one who has begotten. Once again, the things that have been written are in harmony. "From the womb, before the morning star, have I begotten you",[143] the Law says. "The Only-begotten God, the one being in the bosom of the Father, that one has made the Father known",[144] the Gospels tell us. "Bosom" has been said by the Gospels and "womb" has been said by the Law. And so, the lawfully-begotten Son, similar to the one who has begotten him, is proclaimed as being from the womb and from the bosom. The voice of the Gospel testifies: "This is my beloved Son, in whom I am well-pleased".[145] The Psalmist also testifies: "You are my Son; today I have begotten you".[146] Since one voice has been conveyed both then and now and it is only one who has spoken (the one who pronounced it then and the one who has addressed us more recently), the one who has spoken is unchanged.

For lately, when having made this pronouncement, he found himself already having been anticipated and declared beforehand in the Psalms. Additionally, there is a command from the Father to the divine powers to serve the Son and to render reverence and worship to him (for it is written: "And let all the angels of God worship him"[147]).

Paul has agreed with the command — I should say that he works it anew and expounds it and endeavours to become an interpreter of what was said beforehand and what was written beforehand: "For when he introduces the first-born to the whole world he says: 'And let all the angels of God worship him.'"[148] You will even see that the apostle has endeavoured to interpret the ancient things, not by neglecting to describe in detail the things in the Law, but

---

subject-matter at hand, the implied reference to Heb 1:3 seems certain to me.
[140] Deut 6:4.
[141] Mark 10:18 and Luke 18:19. See also Matt 19:17.
[142] 1 Cor 8:6.
[143] Ps 109:3 (110:3).
[144] John 1:18.
[145] Matt 3:17 and 17:5. See also Mark 1:11, 9:7 and Luke 3:22, 9:35.
[146] Ps 2:7.
[147] Ps 96:7 (97:7).
[148] Heb 1:6. Contrary to Casey, who only placed the quotation of Ps 96:7 (97:7) within quotation marks, Fitschen correctly includes: "For when he introduces the First-born to the whole world he says", within the quotations since Sarapion is citing Heb 1:6, which includes the quotation from the Psalm.

at one point saying: "You placed all things under his feet",[149] and immediately explaining: "When it says that all things have been subjugated, it is clear that except for the one who placed all things under him, the Son permitted nothing to be unsubjugated so that God might be all in all",[150] and at another point saying: "Because of this, a man will leave his father and his mother. This is a great mystery, but I say it with respect to Christ and the church".[151]

The apostles are also interpreters of the ancient things, and the ancient things are in harmony with the new things. Or rather, as many as are apostles interpret, but as many as are not apostles speak slanderously. For by not doing what the apostles do, but fighting against what has been written by them, they falsify apostleship, being false prophets. For behold, the eisegetes of truth, having honoured the Law, exegeted the Law, while these people, having slandered the Law, skirmish with the Law and quarrel with those who exegete the Law.[152] The apostles know the exact similarity of the Gospel and the Law and, taking up the Law, they see the Gospel and, looking in the Gospel, they do not rescind the Law, but these people are those who always considered similar things dissimilar and who profess things friendly toward themselves to be implacable hostile sisters. They do not avoid the refutation of evil but, having endeavoured to separate and divide in two the things that are alike (though not being able to divide them in two since the Law does not prove itself to be divided from the Gospel) they reaped the punishment of their malice.

For behold! Whatever things there are concerning the Father in the Law, these also lie in the Gospels. Whatever things there are concerning the Son, these are spoken in both. Whatever things there are concerning the Holy Spirit, these we should be able to find in both. For neither of the two writings forgets the Holy Spirit, but in the Gospel he is the gift, while in the Law he is the request. Indeed, at one point, David says: "Take not your Holy Spirit from me",[153] and at another point the Gospel says: "Receive the Holy Spirit",[154] in order that what one has might not be taken away, but what is given graciously one might possess by receiving. Souls may be honoured through the communion of the Holy Spirit, neither being torn away from the communion nor continuing without the communion. And someone will have power over angels and archangels and the other powers, and over heaven and earth, and

---

[149] Ps 8:6. Quoted in 1 Cor 15:27, but in the third person singular rather than second person singular.

[150] 1 Cor 15:27-28. See also Heb 2:5-8, which used the same passage from Ps 8 in a similar manner.

[151] Eph 5:31-32.

[152] I have chosen to transliterate for *eisegete* in order to emphasise the comparison Sarapion made between eisegeting truth and exegeting the Law. Doing this also assists the reader in noting the circularity at work here.

[153] Ps 50:13 (51:11).

[154] John 20:23.

the other creations when he has investigated [all of this] in order to behold the similarity of the Law and the Gospel, thus extending [this activity] to the smallest detail.

49

We, however, refuse so great a dignity, having only furnished what is needful for the hypothesis, and encouraging those eager for knowledge, who have held fast to the hypothesis, to advance toward all the things that are beheld. What the heretics reproach with some sort of accusation, only this will we also add in argument, so that we might both destroy their accusation and observe the functions of the Law. For if they are the ones perceiving the accusation against the Scriptures, they have a wanton mouth, but we should both put to shame their ignorance with respect to the similarity and not decline to cast aside the accusation.

For they accuse the ancient Law of being harsh and unpleasant, and they accuse the ancient servants of being stricter and of being those who lean more toward punishment, and of being those who have removed themselves from merciful love, since they are not perceiving what has been written: "Mercy and judgment I will sing, with respect to you, Lord".[155]

Having not known that the perfection of the plan of salvation[156] depends upon mercy and punishment and, because of this, being dim-sighted, they are silent concerning the mercies of the Law. Rather, they remember the punishments and cry up and down.

"Do not look", one declares, "where the children abuse Elisha. He cursed them and he gave the children over to be delivered to two bears, having prepared the children to be food, even a meal, for the bears."[157] Do not look", one declares, "where some unwilling soldiers were sent by command to call upon Elijah. The commanding officer hesitated to march and refused to reach Elijah, but Elijah brought down fire, saying: 'If I am a man of God, fire will come down from heaven and consume you and your fifty men,' and it consumed and destroyed the men".[158]

Since they place such invectives and punishments in the category of evil and bad, what will they say concerning Paul? Because once while Bar-Jesus the magician was conversing with Sergius Paulus, the proconsul, St Paul saw how, through the deceitfulness of the discourse, the mind of those being instructed was twisted, he did not tolerate it, but punished it and produced blindness. He cried: "O full of deceit and all fraud, son of the Devil, will you not stop

---

[155] Ps 100:1 (101:1).

[156] Literally, the "economy" (οἰκονομία).

[157] 4 Kgs 2:23-24.

[158] 4 Kgs 1:9-12. Elijah actually performs this action twice, killing two groups of fifty soldiers by means of his declaration.

twisting the straight paths of the Lord? And behold! The hand of the Lord is upon you and you will be blind, not seeing the sun for a period of time.'"[159]

And what will they say concerning Peter, since having judged and questioned Ananias, he caused him to fall dead, and handed over Sappheira to the same tomb (when Ananias and Sappheira, having sold their possessions set aside a portion yet preserved a portion)? For they were dead, having been destroyed by a word.[160]

And so fire, having given heed, consumed those who came, just as a word, having come forth in view of those being taught, caused the ones who peddled the faith to die. And so Elisha handed over the bodies of the youths to the wild beasts just as Paul took away the sight of the eyes and made blind the one who could see. By effecting such things, they have given out punishments.

Therefore, if the punishment is apprehended as wicked, Paul and Peter are wicked. However, if they are good because they are apostles and are good because they have laid down punishment, why do you speak slanderously against the punishments, even with respect to punishments the apostles employed? If we accept the apostles but find fault with the punishments, then the laws do not judge the actions or render judgment against an individual and do not distinguish amongst persons, but lump them together on account of the similarity of their actions.

"But", they say, "the Son is merciful, what is written in the Gospels is merciful, and the one who is merciful, being a child, is from the one who is merciful. But the Law is harsh, not pardoning sinners, but the Gospel has pity, moderating faults and invoking repentance. For behold the Saviour!" They say, "he spared Peter who disowned him and caused to stand beside him the one who has produced so great a sin and pretended to threaten him through his benevolence, having left behind, as an example, the man with his whole life, so that he might present an icon of his benevolence in that man".

What, then, is the Law? Is it in need of a representation and devoid of an appropriate icon? Peter, being a zealous man who has fallen, has been honoured because of remission and forgiveness, but is there no one in the Law who, having erred, and erred greatly, has sought exemption through repentance? For if they are ignorant, we will say what is written: "Have mercy on me, O God, according to your great mercy, and according to the multitude of your compassions, blot out my transgression. Wash me thoroughly from my iniquity and cleanse me from my sin. Against you only have I sinned and committed what is evil before you".[161] If they had known this, they would hold their peace with respect to spoken evil.

---

[159] Acts 13:10-11.
[160] Acts 5:1-11.
[161] Ps 50:1-2, 4 (51:1-2, 4).

50

Therefore the deeds are related. The icons are similar. Here, on the one hand, is Peter and there, on the other hand, is the Psalmist, so the falls of the great men were healed by a great forgiveness. For those who have committed great offences, mercy became great.

Therefore, if they marvel at the Gospels because Peter received mercy, they should marvel that David received mercy. If they should claim that David was not acquitted with as much mercy, then on their account neither will Peter escape blame. One might think the charge is only against David, but in actuality, Peter will be accused by the same charge.

If they say that forgiveness is good, but the forgiveness of the ancient Law extended only as far as one example while, there in the Gospels, there is a plethora of forgiveness and a flood of acquittal, and there is a voice that has cried: "Come to me, all who are weary and heavy-laden and I will give you rest",[162] let them read the ancient things and admit wonder at the things that have been written.

If they refuse to read the writings because of carelessness, let them remove these from this charge. The Saviour says: "Come, all who are weary and heavy-laden and I will give you rest",[163] disregarding no one, abandoning no one, including everyone. The Psalmist says: "All nations, clap your hands",[164] and again: "Listen, all who dwell in the inhabited world, both boorish men and sons of cultivated men, rich and poor together".[165] Everyone has been called forth from the Gospel. Everyone has been called forth from the Law. The Gospel leaves aside no one. The Law disowns no one.

The Gospel cried: "Repent, for the kingdom of heaven has drawn near!"[166] It sent this instruction forth to everyone, spoke to those who stumble, addressed those who have fallen, announced to those who were already bound to death, and solicited freedom through a proclamation. Besides, Jonah lived in Ninevah, not in a small city, but full of people. He made the threat known and did not remain silent about the punishment, but cried out with startling speech. He knew the hostile men and brought them to a change in their position. He caused them to be men free from sin. The punishment that had been announced beforehand was undone. Mercy took its place. What was sought after occurred. For the destruction of the people was not sought, but the change of their ways was sought. And because what was sought occurred and the men changed, the gift of philanthropy appeared. The one who judges,

---

[162] Matt 11:28.
[163] Ibid.
[164] Ps 46:2 (47:1).
[165] Ps 48:1-2 (49:1-2).
[166] Matt 3:2.

being an advocate, cried and said to his servant: "If you had mercy upon the gourd, for which you did not suffer, which came into being by night and perished by night, shall I not show mercy upon the great city Ninevah, in which dwell more than twelve thousand men and many cattle?"[167]

God was merciful and clear, being the one who spoke, who just now said these things, and having cried out through another prophet: "I do not desire the death of a sinner, but that he turn and live".[168] He is the one being praised by those who have learned to sing: "The Lord is compassionate and merciful, long-suffering and full of mercy".[169]

For with God the outpouring of compassion is so great that he does not forbid the smallest, most insignificant and unworthy inclination toward repentance of exceedingly evil men. For when Ahab had nearly been driven on to extreme evils and was pricked by remorse in some way, God requited the penalty and made the circumstances known to his servant and curtailed the threat, abandoning the punishment for an interval of time. He says: "Have you seen how Ahab has been pricked by remorse? I will not bring on the evil in his days, but in other days",[170] so that God might honour even the smallest drops of repentance with a fitting honour.

51

Having made these observations up to now, we have ended this so that their argument concerning the Law might not be completely unaddressed by having been left undisputed, adding in writing only this: that "the Law has the shadow of the good things intended".[171] For a boy-ward assists the child (and the one who is of a young age) until the teacher, getting possession of him, hands on greater instructions. For one will be able to furnish exactly what is needed after establishing this idea as a hypothesis: "The Law came through Moses but grace and truth came from the Lord".[172]

However, we should also apply ourselves to the other attacks of the miscarriage, exposing another absurd notion in its own words and laying the attacks bare by close examinations, so that (if it is even possible) we might be able to free ourselves from the entrapping thoughts of the unreasonable notion.

For it extends even to the work of creation, and this visible work is professed to be a work of deceit and man to be a work of evil, and the soul to be from God, to be joined together with evil. And so the human being has come into existence by having taken the essence of a body from the essence of evil.

---

[167] Jonah 4:10-11.
[168] Ezek 33:11.
[169] Ps 102:8 (103:8).
[170] 3 Kgs 20:29.
[171] Heb 10:1.
[172] John 1:17.

Yet the essence of the soul has been taken back by God like the arms stripped off an enemy or the spoils of war that have been carried off as booty by evil. So, both from what was carried off as booty and from the essence of evil (from soul and body) the human being has come into existence, and evil is not the cause of the soul and has not made the essence of the soul but is only what produces its entrance into the body. For as a plunderer (as they say), evil brought the soul into flesh, but flesh itself and the form itself and the outward appearance and such a shape, indeed, the whole essence, is the work and formation of the deceiver.

Therefore, by confessing that the human being has come into existence from opposing things, they neither know the explanation of opposing things nor that some things concerning opposing things are such: the things are not mixed with each other, and are unable to exhibit any mixture and association with themselves but, by keeping an association, they would be the cause of their own destruction, not being able to be united but the one being destroyed because of the victory of the other.

For behold, day and night would not be found simultaneously in one bedchamber since light alone is found to destroy darkness. Look, self-control and fornication would not be revealed in one soul since self-control alone, being displayed, causes fornication to be far off. Look, godliness and godlessness would not exist in one person at the same time. For when piety is displayed, not a drop of godlessness is revealed. The Apostle confirms and seals the things being said. "What association has light with darkness? What share does Christ have with Beliar?"[173] For things that oppose each other would not be friends with each other, and one harmony could not make things at variance from itself. For neither does one harmony exist from both motion and stillness nor does one communication exist from silence and speaking. For only one thing would exist, the other not remaining united.

If the body was from evil and the soul from God, how are they rendered into the single harmony of a human being? How are they rendered into a single disposition and friendliness? For behold, one human being has been joined together and come into existence and, through harmony, there is one soul. Look, the soul inhabits the body, and likes and loves the body. "For no one ever hates his own flesh, but nourishes and cares for it."[174] If in fact one cares about the other and the soul regards the pain of the body as its own pain and does not separate itself from the sufferings, but reconciles itself to the wounds, reconciles itself to sufferings and, when it suffers pain, it is grieved because of the wounds, then it is unable to be free from pain. And when the body enjoys itself and is roused by malicious pleasure, the soul also participates in

---

[173] 2 Cor 6:15.
[174] Eph 5:29.

the emotions and partakes of the stimulations and ceases in the same manner, making progress in this way, and as the soul removes itself from the emotions of the passions, the body simultaneously ceases and becomes calm. And when desire becomes enflamed in the soul and the stimulations become enflamed, the body takes pleasure and burns. So both the stimulations and the endings and cessations of the stimulations come into being in the same manner.

If humanity was from opposing things and the body was from evil but the soul from God, then in the first place, a union could not occur (much less could a lasting mixture be completed). Second, neither one could accept the other but each one would accept its own things as its own and reckon the things of the other as hostile. The pleasure of the body would not be the pleasure of the soul, nor would the wound of the body produce pain in the soul, but each would keep to itself and its own pleasure and wounds.

How would the Devil be strong enough to seize what is not his own? How would the soul, not being of the Devil but being another's and by no means having any mixture with his realm, but being of another essence (and of an essence completely hostile to evil) be in hostile and strange things? And how would it bear the mixture with the body since it would be a bond with evil and would not be bound to what is its own? And how would it make the flesh its own and make it holy and provide it with virtue so as to portray the potential for something better? For when the body might be pure and clean and spotless, when it might be holy and reverent, when it might possess holy speech, when it might possess righteous speech, when it might possess righteous sight, when it might possess godly emotions, what is this other than what makes it like something better? And so it is adapted to what is good and brings forth an image of something better.

52

And so these things have been said. However, let us add a few more arguments in order that the addition of the arguments might produce humiliation in them but a precision of faith in us. For in the Gospel, the Saviour, remembering the creation of man and woman, and returning creation to his Father, the maker of all, said: "When creating, he made them male and female from the beginning", and said: "Because of this, a man shall leave his father and mother and be joined to his wife and the two shall become one flesh. Therefore, what God has joined together, let no one separate".[175] He knew the aim of the body and the soul, confessing their cause. He confesses the Father and attacks human thinking, desiring that what has been made should be undivided and not permitting anyone to separate, through human reasoning, the things that have been well-joined.

---

[175] Mark 10: 6, 7, and 9.

To those who place their care in appearances and who have neglected hidden things and the care for what lies within, he says in the Gospel: "Fools! Did not the one who made what is external also make what is internal?"[176] If what is within is the soul and what is external is the body, and the one who has made what is within has made the soul and the one who has made what is external has made the body, the Creator of the soul would also be the Creator of the body and God is the one who makes both and joins and binds them together, the one who has joined together this most holy harmony.

The Saviour himself makes it clear in his own discourse what sort of care he has for the body, when he says: "There are eunuchs who have made themselves eunuchs for the kingdom of heaven. Let the one who is able to comprehend this accept it".[177] For by having exhibited this concern for the body and by preparing it to be holy and dispassionate and without pleasure, and by guarding it and cutting off every desire by his discourse, he exhibits concern for the body and indicates care for the flesh.

And having concern and giving heed to the matter, he preaches because of concern, extending his preaching even to sight so that while the sight is being employed, it might not happen to be filled with sordidness and defilement, but through the body and the soul having been joined together, it might remain as vigorous as possible. For he says in the Gospel: "Whoever looks upon a woman with desire has already committed adultery in his heart".[178]

And so he attributes the passion in the body to the heart and, in that he concerns himself with seeing, he makes it a common concern with the heart, having introduced the passion of the act of seeing as a passion of the heart, and placing concern for the eyes together with a concern for thinking. For the eye does harm in no other way than how the mind does harm. For the eye cannot be perverted unless the soul is perverted. For when the soul is reasonable and seeing straight, the eyes will see suitably. So then, having despised the wicked sight, he introduces holy sight so that "the eyes may see straight and the eyelids might beckon toward righteous things".[179] For he lifts up the eyes, not allowing them to be guided by themselves, but arousing them and exciting them and preparing them for exalting themselves. So having a great concern for bodies, he has both borne a body and entered a body.

53

If, therefore, he did not enter into a body, what do they say concerning the cross and the marks of the nails and the mark of the spear and the tomb and

---

[176] Luke 11:40
[177] Matt 19:12.
[178] Matt 5:28.
[179] Prov 4:25.

the burial? If, being refuted by these things, they confess that the Saviour took on a body, what will they be saying other than saying he has been formed by evil, and no longer is it only a human body that is from evil, but even the body of the Benefactor? For will they not desist until they reach this opinion and lash out with their tongue against the Saviour? For the one endeavouring to argue against those things borne by the Saviour sharpens the tongue only to argue against himself.

The Saviour was washed in the Jordan in baptism, purified in water[180]—and who does he happen to be? For if he neither bears nor possesses a body, what is in common between spiritual beings and rivers? Who among the angels, which power, which dominion, which ruler, which authority, has descended into a place of bathing and was able to experience water? For if neither a power nor an authority nor any throne…went down into the water,[181] the deed has not been examined and what is examined has become both manifest and visible.

Yet, he rose from the water, was tried by the Devil, hungered, thirsted, sailed by sea, slept, travelled, grew tired, walked slowly and, being famished, went to the fig tree. Lastly, he suffered, was crucified. What do these facts cry out? What do these things testify? Let tongues be silenced! Let the actions speak! The deeds possess a mouth. While no longer expending air, let us send forth what has been conveyed. The Scriptures have a mouth. Even if we were silent, the deeds are not silent. Even if we did not speak, the Scriptures do not refrain from speaking.

Therefore, since these things possess the ability to witness in this way, and the actions are trustworthy and the words concerning the actions are true, and the force of the actions cries out that the Saviour possessed a body, even a mortal body, and that he bore the body for our sake and he further sought after what was like it, then the Creator of that one and the Creator of our own has come for our sake. For if it were another, he should not have provided a provision for the others from that one. If, however, it has been made, and has been made by God, it has been made for us; it was made for his own. For in order that he might save his own, he made that one, effecting the freedom of all of his own by making that one. Therefore, thanksgiving is due to the one who has created our bodies, the one who has providentially cared for the ones who have, themselves, acted heedlessly. And to the one who sent his own Son in a body and gave it as a pledge for our bodies so that we might no longer bend down and cast our eyes to the ground, but might be straightened through the communion of the bodies.

Therefore let us disparage those deceivers through this because they have

---

[180] Mark 1:9-11; Matt 3:13-17; Luke 3:21-22; John 1:29-34.
[181] Col. 1:16. Throne is a rank of angel. Here, Sarapion is using Col 1:16 to argue that no rank of angel descended into the River Jordan.

proceeded against bodies and advanced against the Creator and stretched out their tongue against God's plan of salvation,[182] and have not ceased to speak with their tongue against our freedom, being vagabonds and vulgar men who have gathered a collection of evil words. For it is possible for one thing that is expelled to be censured and then another, but having proceeded against everything in order, it is deemed useless and strange to continue. Because of this, we, returning to their whole argument, should not grant much significance to their argument. Let us stand firm against these with a few more words, both having furnished a refutation through the things said above and having indicated other things.

For those who are earnest, care is necessary so that, having surpassed every deception, they might keep their ears unassailable by evil. Thus they might be key keepers of their ears and those who open when the true Word knocks but close when the lying and deceptive word, pretending to be the truth, hastens to enter into the hidden room of the mind. "For many who have disguised themselves and changed their appearance knock at the ears saying, 'I am the Christ,' and will lead many astray."[183]

Yet there is only one Christ, the one who frees, the triumphant one, the benefactor, the one knocking with purpose, the one who brings about our freedom by his entrance, who at the same time expels sins by his entrance, the one who gives love to the Father through his entrance, the one who immediately upon his entrance sets up monuments of the victory over evil, the one who places his beneficence in the soul. If this one should enter and be within, godly and reverent festivals occur, dances that cannot be described, a rejoicing honoured in silence. For, immediately, he draws up the mind, excites the soul, and makes it something uplifted toward better things.

Certainly, when someone sees that, he no longer looks to himself but is amazed by the beauty beheld. Everything else is regarded as ugly. Because of that beneficence, he cries: "Vanity of vanity; everything is vanity",[184] crying: "I consider all things as refuse in order that I may gain Christ".[185] Consequently, when he knocks in such a manner, the mind slows down and is provided with sleep, and that he might become the cause of the sleepiness, he sends forth a pronouncement ("Open to me, my sister, my bride, because my head is filled with dew and my locks of hair with the drops of the night")[186] so that he might exhibit friendship and show care. Because the Word, when being shut out, holds up and bears being outside, and he does not remove himself until the mind should open itself due to the persistence of the asking and the knocking,

---

[182] Literally, "economy"; (οἰκονομία).
[183] Matt 24:5.
[184] Eccl 1:2.
[185] Phil 3:8.
[186] Song 5:2.

providing a place for himself because of the knocking.[187]

54

The enchanters, the false prophets, and false Christs go about, knocking anywhere and burrowing in anywhere. They make use of gentle rapping and mimic the true knocking. Quickly the mind, being deceived by the similarity of the knocking, opens as for a fellow resident or acquaintance. Not having declined to dig through a wall like a thief, but having made haste to dig through so that they might certainly capture the thoughts by deceit or force, some they took by force and some they have beguiled with deceit.

On account of this, the wise and pious are the keepers of the keys, having combined knowledge with vigilance. They have never been burrowed into because of keeping watch. They have never been deceived because of knowledge. For knowledge brings about vigilance and vigilance does not allow a place for those who dig through. For this reason, let us, being wise and pious, keep the keys of our own minds, vanquishing deceit through knowledge and seeking inviolability for ourselves through vigilance.

---

[187] See Luke 12:36; John 10:3; and Rev 3:20. There may also be a reference to Luke 11:9 implied.

Select Bibliography

Primary Sources

Alexander of Lycopolis   *Critique of the Doctrines of the Manichaeans.* Augustus Brinkmann (ed.), *Alexandri Lycopolitani Contra Manichaei opiniones disputatio* 1895 (repr., Stuttgart: Teubner, 1989).

Alexander of Lycopolis   *Critique of the Doctrines of Manichaeus.* In P.W. van der Horst, and J. Mansfeld (transls. and eds.), *An Alexandrian Platonist Against Dualism: Alexander of Lycopolis' Treatise 'Critique of the Doctrines of Manichaeus'.* (Leiden: Brill, 1974).

Athanasius   *Festal Epistle* 12. In William Cureton (ed.), *The Festal Letters of Athanasius* (London: Society for the Publication of Oriental Texts, 1848).

Athanasius   *Festal Epistle* 12. PG 26, 1412–13, Latin Translation.

Athanasius   *Letters on the Holy Spirit.* PG 26, 525–676.

Athanasius   *Letters on the Holy Spirit.* C.R.B. Shapland (trans.), *The Letters of Saint Athanasius Concerning the Holy Spirit* (London: Epworth, 1951).

Athanasius   *Life of Anthony.* G.J.M. Bartelink (ed. and trans.), *Athanase d'Alexandrie: Vie d'Antoine* (SC 400; Paris: Éditions du Cerf, 1994).

Athanasius   *Life of Anthony.* Robert C. Gregg (trans.), *Athanasius: The Life of Anthony and the Letter to Marcellinus* (New York: Paulist, 1980).

Cassian, John   *Collationes XIII* (Michael Petschenig, ed.; Text of the collationes reproduced from 1886 ed.; CSEL 13; Wien: Verlag der Österreichischen Akademie der Wissenschaften, 2004).

Cassian, John   *Conferences* (Colm Luibheid, trans.; New York: Paulist, 1985).

Desert Fathers   Benedicte Ward, *The Sayings of the Desert Fathers, the Alphabetical Collection* (Kalamazoo: Cistercian, 1975).

Epictetus   *Discourses.* W.A. Oldfather (trans.), *Epictetus, the Discourses as Reported by Arrian, the Manual, and Fragments* (LCL 131; 2 Vols.; London and New York: Heinemann and Harvard University Press, 1926).

Epictetus   *Encheiridion.* W.A. Oldfather (trans.), *Epictetus, the Discourses as Reported by Arrian, the Manual, and Fragments* (LCL 131; London and New York: Heinemann and Harvard University Press, 1926), Volume 2.

Gregory of Nyssa	*Against Apollinarius*. Friedrich Mueller (ed.), *Gregorii Nysseni Opera* (Leiden: Brill, 1958), 131–233.
Jerome	*Letters*. Isidorus Hilberg (ed.); *Sancti Eusebii Hieronymi Epistulae* (Vienna: Verlag der Österreichischen Akademie der Wissenschaften, 1996).
Jerome	*On Illustrious Men* (Thomas P. Halton, trans.; Washington, DC: Catholic University of America, 1999).
Pachomius:	Armand Veilleux (trans.), *Pachomian Koinonia. Vol. 1: The Life of Pachomius and His Disciples* (Cistercian Studies, no. 45; Kalamazoo: Cistercian, 1980).
Papyri:	Roberts, C.H. (ed.) *Catalogue of the Greek and Latin Papyri in the John Rylands Library*, Manchester, vol 3, Theological and literary texts, nos 457–551 (Manchester: Manchester University Press, 1938).
Phileas:	Albert Pietersma (ed. and trans.), *The Acts of Phileas, Bishop of Thmuis (Including Fragments of the Greek Psalter)* (Geneva: Patrick Cramer, 1984).
Sarapion of Thmuis	*Against the Manichaeans*. Robert Pierce Casey, "Serapion of Thmuis Against the Manichees." *Harvard Theological Studies* 15 (1931). Published as an extra number of the *Harvard Theological Review*.
Sarapion of Thmuis	*Euchologion*. Dmitrievskii, A. "Евхологион IV века Сарапиона, епископа Тмуитскаго." Труды, Киевской духовной академии 2 (1894), 242–274.
Sarapion of Thmuis	*Letter to Eudoxios*. PG 40.924–5.
Sarapion of Thmuis	*Letter on the Death of Anthony*. In Outtier, B. with A. Louf, M. Van Prys, and Cl.-A. Zirnheld, *Lettres des pères du désert: Ammonas, Macaire, Arsène, Sérapion de Thmuis. Spiritualité Orientale* 42 (Bégrolles en Mauges, Maine & Loire: Abbaye de Bellefontaine, 1985. Also in René Draguet, "Une letter de Sérapion de Thmuis aux disciples d'Antoine (A.D. 356) en version syriaque et arménienne," *Le Muséon* 64 (1951), 1–25.
Sarapion of Thmuis	*Letter to the Monks*. PG 40.925–41.
Sarapion of Thmuis	*Prayers:* Maxwell E. Johnson (trans.), *The Prayers of Sarapion of Thmuis: A Literary, Liturgical, and Theological Analysis* (OCA 249; Rome: Pontifical Oriental Institute, 1995).
Sozomen	*Ecclesiastical History*. J. Bidez and G.C. Hansen (eds.), *Historia ecclesiastica* (GCS 50; Berlin: de Gruyter, 1960).

Sozomen — *Ecclesiastical History.* Edward Walford (trans.), *The Ecclesiastical History of Sozomen, Comprising a History of the Church from A.D. 324 to A.D. 440. Translated from the Greek: with a Memoir of the Author. Also the Ecclesiastical History of Philostorgius, as Epitomised by Photius (*London: Henry G. Bohn, 1855).

Secondary Sources

Anatolios, Kahled — *Athanasius. The Coherence of his Thought* (London: Routledge, 2004).

Ataç, Mehmet-Ali — "Manichaeism and Ancient Mesopotamian 'Gnosticism'", *Journal of Ancient Near Eastern Religions* 5:1 (2005), 1–39.

Barrett-Lennard, R.J.S. — *The Sacramentary of Sarapion of Thmuis: A Text for Students, with Introduction, Translation, and Commentary* (Bramcote, England: Joint Liturgical Studies, 1993).

Baumeister, Theofried — "Der ägyptische Bischof und Märtyrer Phileas," in Maria-Barbara von Stritzky and Christian Uhrigg (eds.), *Garten des Lebens: Festschrift für Winfrid Cramer* (Altenberge: Oros, 1999), 33–41.

BeDuhn, David — *The Manichaean Body* (Baltimore and London: Johns Hopkins University Press, 2000).

Behr, John — *The Nicene Faith.* Part 2 (Crestwood, New York: St Vladimir's Seminary Press, 2004).

Behr, John — *The Way to Nicaea* (Crestwood, New York: St Vladimir's Seminary Press, 2003).

Bell, H. Idris (ed.) — *Jews and Christians in Egypt: The Jewish Troubles in Alexandria and the Athanasian Controversy, Illustrated by Texts from Greek Papyri in the British Museum* (Westport, CT: Greenwood Press, 1972 [Original: 1924]).

Botte, Bernard — "L'Eucologe de Serapion est-il authentique," *Oriens Christianus* 48 (1964), 50–6.

Brennan, Brian — "Athanasius' Vita Antonii, a Sociological Interpretation," *Vigiliae Christianae* 39 (1985), 209–27.

Brennan, Tad — "Stoic Moral Psychology," in Brad Inwood (ed.), *The Cambridge Companion to the Stoics* (Cambridge: Cambridge University Press, 2003), 257–294.

Brightman, F.E. — "The Sacramentary of Serapion," *Journal of Theological Studies* 1 (1900), 88–113, 247–77.

Bruns, J. Edgar "Ammonius Sakkas and Ammonius of Thmuis," *Sciences Religieuses* 4:4 (1975), 387–91.

Burton-Christie, Douglas *The Word in the Desert: Scripture and the Quest for Holiness in Early Christian Monasticism* (Oxford: Oxford University Press, 1993).

Casey, Robert Pierce "Serapion of Thmuis Against the Manichees," *Harvard Theological Studies* 15 (1931). Published as an extra number of the *Harvard Theological Review*.

Casey, Robert Pierce "The Text of the Anti-Manichaean Writings of Titus of Bostra and Serapion of Thmuis," *Harvard Theological Review* 21 (1928), 97–111.

Cattaneo, Enrico "Review of B. Outtier, with A. Louf, M. Van Prys, and Cl.-A. Zirnheld, *Lettres des pères du désert: Ammonas, Macaire, Arsène, Sérapion de Thmuis*", *Orientalia Christiana Periodica* 52:1 (1986), 240–1.

Colish, Marcia *The Stoic Tradition from Antiquity to the Early Middle Ages. Vol. 2. Stoicism in Christian Latin Thought through the Sixth Century* (Leiden: Brill, 1985).

Daley, Brian "Apokatastasis and 'Honorable Silence' in the Eschatology of Maximus the Confessor." In Felix Heinzer and Christoph von Schönborn (eds.), *Maximus Confessor: Actes du Symposium sur Maxime le Confesseur Fribourg, 2–5 septembre 1980* (Fribourg: Éditions Universitaire, 1982), 309–339.

Devreesse, Robert *Les anciens commentateurs grecs de l'Octateque et des Rois: (fragments tirés des chaines)* (Vatican City: Biblioteca Apostolica Vaticana, 1959).

Dmitrievskii, A. "Евхологион IV века Сарапиона, епископа Тмуитскаго." Труды Киевской духовной академии 2 (1894), 242–274.

Draguet, René "Une letter de Sérapion de Thmuis aux disciples d'Antoine, (A.D. 356) en version syriaque et arménienne," *Le Muséon* 64 (1951), 1–25.

Évieux, Pierre "Review of B. Outtier, with A. Louf, M. Van Prys, and Cl.-A. Zirnheld, *Lettres des pères du désert: Ammonas, Macaire, Arsène, Sérapion de Thmuis*", *Recherches de science religieuse* 77:3 (1989), 420–1.

Fitschen, Klaus *Serapion von Thmuis: Echte und Unechte Schriften sowie die Zeugnisse des Athanasius und Anderer* (Berlin and New York: de Gruyter, 1992).

Fitzgerald, John T.   *Cracks in an Earthen Vessel: An Examination of the Catalogues of Hardships in the Corinthian Correspondence* (SBLDS 99; Atlanta: SBL, 1986).

Frankfurter, David   "The Cult of the Martyrs in Egypt before Constantine," *Vigiliae Christianae* 48 (1994), 25–47.

Frankfurter, David   *Elijah in Upper Egypt: The Apocalypse of Elijah and Early Egyptian Christianity* (SAC; Minneapolis: Fortress, 1993).

Franzmann, Majella   *Jesus in the Manichaean Writings* (London: Bloomsbury, 2003).

Funk, F.X.   *Didascalia et Constitutiones Apostolorum,* vol. 2 (Paderborn: in Libraria Ferdinandi Schoeningh, 1905).

Gardner, Iain, and Samuel N.C. Lieu   *Manichaean Texts from the Roman Empire* (Cambridge: Cambridge University Press, 2004).

Globe, Alexander   "Serapion of Thmuis as Witness to the Gospel Text used by Origen in Caesarea," *Novum Testamentum* 26:2 (1984), 97–127.

Goehring, James E.   *Ascetics, Society, and the Desert, Studies in Early Egyptian Monasticism* (Harrisburg, Pennsylvania: Trinity Press International, 1999).

Gonnet, Dominique   "The salutary action of the Holy Spirit as proof of his divinity in Athanasius' Letters to Serapion." In Maurice F. Wiles (ed.), *Studia Patristica: Papers Delivered at the International Conference on Patristic Studies.* Vol. 36 (Leuven: Peeters, 2001).

Griggs, C. Wilfred   *Early Egyptian Christianity, from its Origins to 451 C.E.* (Coptic Studies, 2; Leiden: Brill, 1991).

Grillmeier, Aloys, in collaboration with Theresia Hainthaler   *Christ in Christian Tradition Volume 2, part 2: The Church of Constantinople in the sixth century* (John Cawte and Pauline Allen, transls.; Atlanta: John Knox, 1995 [1986]).

Hart, David B.   *The Beauty of the Infinite: the Aesthetics of Christian Truth* (Grand Rapids: Eerdmans, 2003.

Haykin, Michael, A.G.   *The Spirit of God: The Exegesis of 1 and 2 Corinthians in the Pneumatomachian Controversy of the Fourth Century* (Leiden, New York, and Köln: Brill, 1994).

Herbel, Dellas Oliver   "A 'Doctrine of Scripture' from the Eastern Orthodox Tradition: A Reflection on the Desert Father Sarapion of Thmuis." In Matthew Baker and Mark Mourachian (eds.), *What Is the Bible?: The Patristic Doctrine of Scripture* (Minneapolis: Fortress, 2016), 21–34.

Irwin, T.H. "Stoic Naturalism and its Critics." In Brad Inwood (ed.), *The Cambridge Companion to the Stoics* (Cambridge: Cambridge University Press, 2003), 345–364.

Johnson, Maxwell E. "A Fresh Look at the Prayers of Sarapion of Thmuis," *Studia Liturgica* 22:2 (1992), 163–83.

Johnson, Maxwell E. "Review of R.J.S. Barrett-Lennard, *The Sacramentary of Sarapion of Thmuis: A Text for Students, with Introduction, Translation, and Commentary*," *Worship* 69 (1995), 187–90.

Kannengiesser, Charles *Handbook of Patristic Exegesis: The Bible in Ancient Christianity*. Volume 2 (Leiden: Brill, 2004).

Kelley, David "'Apokatastasis' in the Early Church," *Patristic and Byzantine Review* 9:1 (1990), 71–4.

Kettler, F. H. "Der melitianische Streit in Ägypten," *Zeitschrift für die neutestamentliche Wissenschaft und die Kunde der Urchristentums* 35 (1936), 155–93.

Lieu, Samuel N.C. *Manichaeism in the Later Roman Empire and Medieval China* (Tübingen: Mohr, 1992).

Lorenz, Rudolf "Eine Serapion von Thumis [sic] zugeschriebene arabische Vita Antonii," *Zeitscrift fur Kirchengeschichte* 102 (1991), 348–61.

McNary-Zak, Bernadette *Letters and Asceticism in Fourth-Century Egypt* (Lanham, MD: University Press of America, 2000).

Musurillo, Herbert *The Acts of the Christian Martyrs* (Oxford: Oxford University Press, 1972).

Norris, Frank "Universal Salvation in Origen and Maximus." In Nigel M. De S. Cameron (ed.), *Universalism and the Doctrine of Hell* (Carlisle: Paternoster Press; Grand Rapids: Baker, 1992), 35–72.

Oort, Johannes van (ed.) *Manichaeism and Early Christianity: Selected Papers from the 2019 Pretoria Congress and Consultation* (Leiden and Boston: Brill, 2020).

Pedersen, Nils Arne *Demonstrative Proof in Defence of God: A Study of Titus of Bostra's Contra Manichaeos, the Work's Sources, Aims and Relation to its Contemporary Theology* (Leiden and Boston: Brill, 2004).

Perkins, Judith *The Suffering Self: Pain and Narrative Representation in the Early Christian Era* (London and New York: Routledge, 1994).

Peters, A.   "Het Tractaat van Serapion van Thmuis tegen de Manichaeën," *Sacris Erudiri* 2 (1949), 55–94.

Pettersen, Alvyn   "Athanasius' Presentation of Anthony of the Desert's Admiration for his Body," *Studia Patristica* 21 (1989), 438–47.

Quasten, Johannes   *Patrology. Volume 3: The Golden Age of Greek Patristic Literature: From the Council of Nicaea to the Council of Chalcedon* (Reissue edition; Allen, Texas: Ave Maria Press, 1986).

Reeves, John C.   *Heralds of that Good Realm: Syro-Mesopotamian Gnosis and Jewish Traditions* (Leiden and New York: Brill, 1996).

Riggi, C.   "Una testimonianza del "kerygma" cristiano in Alessandro di Licopoli", *Salesianum* 31 (1969), 561–628.

Rist, John M.   "Prohairesis: Proclus, Plotinus, et alii." In Olivier Reverdin (ed.), *De Jamblique a Proclus* (Vandœuvres & Geneva: Fondation Hardt, 1975).

Rodopoulos, Panteleimon   "Doctrinal Teaching in the Sacramenary of Serapion of Thmuis," *Greek Orthodox Theological Review* 9:2 (1963–64), 201–14.

Rubenson, Samuel   *The Letters of St. Anthony: Monasticism and the Making of a Saint* (Minneapolis: Fortress, 1995).

Saake, Helmut   "Das Präskript zum ersten Serapionsbrief des Athanasios von Alexandreia als Pneumatologisches Programm," *Vigiliae Christianae* 26 (1972), 188–99.

Sachs, John R. S.J.   "Apocatastasis in Patristic Theology," *Theological Studies* 54:4 (1993), 617–640.

Schofield, Malcom   "Stoic Ethics." In Brad Inwood (ed.), *The Cambridge Companion to the Stoics* (Cambridge: Cambridge University Press, 2003), 233–256.

Scibona, Concetta Giuffré   "How Monotheistic is Mani's Dualism? Once more on monotheism and dualism in Manichaean gnosis," *Numen: International Review for the History of Religions* 48:4 (2001), 444–67.

Sedley, David   "The School, from Zeno to Arius Didymus." In Brad Inwood (ed.), *The Cambridge Companion to the Stoics* (Cambridge: Cambridge University Press, 2003), 7–32.

Silverman, David P.   "Divinity and Deities in Ancient Egypt." In Byron E. Shafer (ed.), *Religion in Ancient Egypt: Gods, Myths, and Personal Practice* (Ithaca and London: Cornell University Press, 1991), 7–87.

Spinks, Bryan D. "The Integrity of the Anaphora of Sarapion of Thmuis and Liturgical Methodology," *Journal of Theological Studies* 49 (1998), 136–44.

Stowers, Stanley K. *Letter Writing in Greco-Roman Antiquity* (Philadelphia: Westminster John Knox, 1986).

Stroumsa, Gedaliahu G. "The Manichaean Challenge to Egyptian Christianity." In Birger A. Pearson and James E. Goehring (eds.), *The Roots of Egyptian Christianity* (SAC; Philadelphia: Fortress, 1986), 307–319.

Tardieu, Michel *Le Manichéisme* (Paris: Presses Universitaires de France, 1981).

Tezt, Martin "Athanasius und die Vita Antonii: Literarische und theologische Relationen," *Zeitschrift für die neutestamentliche Wissencraft und die Kunde der alteran Kirche* 73 (1982), 1–30.

West, Maxine "The law, a holy school, Serapion of Thmuis and Scripture." In Maurice F. Wiles & E. J. Yarnold (eds.), *Studia Patristica: Papers Delivered at the International Conference on Patristic Studies*. Vol. 35 (Louvain: Peeters, 2001), 198–202.

White, Michael J. "Stoic Natural Philosophy [Physics and Cosmology]." In Brad Inwood (ed.), *The Cambridge Companion to the Stoics* (Cambridge: Cambridge University Press, 2003), 124–152.

Widengren, Geo *Mani and Manichaeism* (Charles Kessler, transl.; London: Weidenfeld and Nicholson, 1965).

Wobbermin, Georg *Altchristliche liturgische Stücke aus der Kirche Aegyptens nebst einem dogmatischen Brief des Bischofs Serapion von Thmuis* (Leipzig and Berlin: J.C. Hinrichs'sche Buchhandlung, 1898).

Young, Frances *Biblical Exegesis and the Formation of Christian Culture* (Cambridge: Cambridge University Press, 1997).

Young, Frances "Alexandrian and Antiochian Exegesis." In Alan J. Hauser and Duane F. Watson (eds.), *A History of Biblical Interpretation. Vol. 1: The Ancient Period* (Grand Rapids: Eerdmans, 2003), 334–354.

Indices

General Index

Aaron, OT figure	63, 79
Abraham, OT figure	61–63, 79, 84, 115–116, 130
abyss	24–25, 106–107
Adam, OT figure	17, 62, 83–84
Adiaphora	29, 44, 47, 55, 70–71
Against the Manichaeans	13–15, 17–41, 43, 44, 53, 55, 59, 60, 65, 67–68, 70–71, 78, 82, 84–85, 89–142
Ahab, OT figure	136
Alexander of Lycopolis	13, 16–18
Alexandria	5–6, 10–12, 14, 26–28, 36, 51–56, 58, 68, 71, 78
Alexandrians	37–38
patriarchate of	16
allegory	36–38, 62, 64
Ambrose of Milan	26
Ammonius Sakkas (Thmuis?)	6
Amoun, ascetic	66, 70, 85
Ananias, NT figure	134
angel(s)	104, 140
Anthony, the Great, of the Desert	ix, 5, 6, 7, 8, 50, 61, 65–67, 69, 70, 79, 85
Antioch	36
Antiochenes	34, 36–38
baptismal ordines of	10
Apocalypse of Elijah	44, 56–58, 71
apokatastasis	13, 26
Apollinarius of Laodicaea	6, 32–33
Apostle	30, 51, 77, 86, 95, 117, 126, 131, 137. See also Paul.
Apostles	17, 23, 51, 62, 84, 86, 95, 99, 101–103, 115, 132, 134
apostleship	103, 132
Arianism	12
Ariston of Chios	29
Armenian translations	13, 68
army	48–49, 69, 84, 99
Athanasius	ix, 6–8, 10–12, 17, 35, 38, 57, 58
Augustine of Hippo	14, 26, 34, 39–41
Bar–Jesus, musician	133
Beatitudes	62

Bible	15, 19, 20–21, 35–38, 60–65
body, human	12, 13, 25, 30–33, 39, 45, 83, 84, 91, 92, 93–94, 97, 101, 104, 129, 136–140
canon	38
child(ren)	45–47, 80, 105–106, 121, 128, 133, 134, 136.
China	12, 13
Chrysippus	29
Clement of Alexandria	10, 26, 35
Coenobium	7
conflagration	14, 43
Constantius II	6
courage	24, 50–52, 54, 59, 62–63, 82, 86, 99, 125, 128–130
cowardice	19, 24, 26, 100, 109, 124–126, 130
darkness (Manichaean)	12–13, 105, 120–121, 137
David, psalmist	21, 50, 62–63, 82–84, 86, 101, 116–117, 121, 132, 135
death	28, 34, 41–45, 47–48, 75, 79–80, 83, 93–95, 135–136
demon(s)	8, 13, 25–27, 48, 62, 69, 83–85, 99, 100, 105–107, 119, 123, 126
Desert Fathers	63–65, 69–72
Diocletian, emperor	14
disease	45, 48, 85
dualism	12, 16, 30–31, 34–35, 39–41
dualistic	12, 41
economies (of Christ)	21–23, 32, 34, 38, 65, 133, 141
Ecumenical Council	26
Second (381)	6
Fifth (553)	26
Egypt	5, 8–9, 14, 17, 55–58, 70–71, 78, 121, 127
Egyptians	44, 129
eisegesis	132
Elijah, prophet	44, 56–58, 71, 78, 115, 133
Elisha, OT figure	94, 99, 133–134
Encomium	65, 67, 69–72
endurance	42, 47, 51–52, 54–55, 59, 60, 70, 75, 77, 81, 86, 98, 102, 119
Epictetus	27, 29, 31, 45–46, 48–49, 52, 54–55
eschaton	46, 55
ethics	24, 27, 29
Euchologion	9
Eusebius of Caesarea	14
Evagrius of Pontus	26
Eve, OT figure	13, 83
evil	13, 18, 24–25, 28, 33, 35, 39–41, 42, 75, 83, 85–86, 89–94, 96, 98, 101–102, 104–114, 119–125, 128, 130, 133–134,

	136–138, 140–141
exegesis	10, 18, 35–38, 121
faith	x, 12, 22, 30, 33, 38, 48, 50–51, 63, 77, 84–86, 92, 115–116, 122, 128–129, 134, 138
faithful	129, 63, 65
Fall	26, 28, 31, 38, 41, 63
falling	28, 39, 42, 56, 69, 75, 81, 101, 111, 112, 123, 129, 134
Family	45–46, 57, 61, 77, 79–80
Faustus, Manichaean	14
Festal Letter	6
fire	28, 42, 43, 75, 85, 89, 106–107, 133–134
freedom	28, 32, 80, 83, 92, 93, 94, 105, 129, 135, 141
free will	18, 26–28, 34, 40–41, 52, 90–93, 95–97, 100–101, 103, 105–108
Gabriel, archangel	117
Gehazi, OT figure	99
Gnosticism	15
Judeo–Christian	15
Gregory, Nazianzus, the Theologian	26, 70
Gregory of Nyssa	26, 28, 33–35
Hades. See Hell	
heedlessness	x, 29, 31–32, 41, 51–53, 86, 92, 94–95, 97–98, 128, 140
hell	26, 78, 85
hermeneutics	ix, 19–41, 59–63
Holy Spirit	14–16, 85, 87, 91, 101, 132
hope	50, 62, 86, 92, 126, 129
illness	42, 47, 75, 80, 94
imprudence	24, 29, 31, 105, 124–126
injustice	26, 119, 124–128
intemperance	26, 124–125
Irenaeus of Lyons	10, 38
Isaiah, prophet	22, 85, 102, 111, 116, 120
Jeremiah, prophet	63
Jerome	16, 70
Jesus	13, 15, 18, 22, 25, 30, 53, 60–62, 64, 70, 77, 89–90, 95–96, 100, 102, 106–107, 114–118, 120, 124, 128
Jews	20, 71, 116, 128
Job	54, 63, 79, 84
John "the maimed"	66
John Cassian	7, 61, 71, 79
John of Lycopolis	66
John the Baptiser	63, 84
John the Persian	63

Jonah, OT figure	100, 135–136
Jordan, river	121, 140
Joseph, OT figure	129
Judas, NT figure	24, 101, 121
Judith, OT figure	129
Justin Martyr	10
Justinian, emperor	26
Kingdoms:	
Two kingdoms (Light, Darkness)	12–13
Kingdom of God	41, 54, 55, 82, 85
Kingdom of Heaven	22, 28, 64, 85, 100, 135, 139
Kingdom of Jesus Christ	115, 117
Law	18–24, 35–36, 65, 69, 77, 79, 81–82, 94, 97, 104, 114–136
Leontius of Byzantium	6
Letter on the Death of Anthony	7, 8, 67–69
Letter to Bishop Eudoxius	ix, 7, 34, 42–43, 69–71, 75, 82, 84
Letter to the Monks	ix, 8, 34, 44–72, 77–87
Letters to Sarapion concerning the Divinity of the Holy Spirit	15
Life of Anthony	6–8, 65–66, 70
light	12–13, 51, 78, 83, 86, 91, 105, 109–110, 112–113, 116–117, 120–121, 125, 137
Lycopolis	5, 13, 16, 66
Macarius, ascetic	66, 70, 85
Macrina, Cappadocian	26
Mani	12, 14, 90, 119–120
Manichaeans	7, 12–41, 90, 93, 94, 99, 108, 116, 118, 119
Marcion, heretic	14, 90, 120
	Marcionites 13, 14, 118
martyrs	5–6, 44, 57–58, 62, 71, 84
Mary, mother of Jesus	117
Matthew, evangelist	23, 62, 116
Maximus the Confessor	26, 28
Melitius, Egyptian bishop	6
Methodius of Olympus	26
Milan	6
mind	33, 35, 41, 77, 89, 91, 93–94, 96, 98–101, 104, 123–127, 131, 133, 139, 141–142
monks	44–72, 77–83
Morning Star	112, 131

Moses, OT figure	21, 63, 79, 115–116, 122, 136
Nebuchadnezzar, OT figure	103–104
neo–Platonism	22
Nicene community of Thmuis	10
Nile river, East Delta of	7
Ninevah	135–136
Old Testament	14, 16, 19, 23, 34
Ophanius, heretic	90
oracle(s)	19–21, 23, 25, 34, 38, 58, 93, 94, 104, 112, 116, 125
Origen	5, 10, 17, 26, 35, 37, 51
Origenism	35, 36
Palestine	26
Paphnutius, ascetic	61, 79
passion	33, 51, 92–93, 98, 105, 127–129, 139
Paul, apostle	40–41
Pelagianism	40–41
Pesher	64
Peter, apostle	10, 22, 30, 63, 94, 100–101, 134–135
Peter II, bishop of Alexandria	15
Pharaoh	44, 55–59, 71, 103–104
Phileas of Thmuis	11
Photius, patriarch of Constantinople	6, 16
Plutarch	29
Pneumatomachi	7, 10, 11, 12
Poemen, ascetic	50, 70
polytheism	123
proficiens/proficientes	44, 49, 52, 53, 55, 56, 58, 59, 65, 69–71
prohairesis	27–28, 53
Prophets	22–24, 62, 65, 84, 89, 114–115, 117–118, 120, 128, 130, 132, 142
providence	37, 115
prudence	24, 50, 85, 97–98, 105, 128–130
purgative inclusivism	26
reincarnation	14, 26
righteousness	24, 51, 54, 82, 87, 128–130
rule	38, 117
Saints	30, 55–57, 79, 93–94, 101, 115
Sappheira, NT figure	134
Satan. See Devil self–control	24, 25, 29, 31–32, 52, 53, 91–94, 96–99, 106, 125, 128–129, 137

Seneca	48–50
Sergius Paulus, proconsul	133
Severian of Gabala	13
sickness	28, 33, 42–43, 47–48, 69–70, 75, 80, 90–91, 94, 98–99, *101*, 111–112
sin	13, 26–28, 33, 42, 43, 69–70, 75, 79, 83, 95–96, 125, 127, 134–135
Sitanus, heretic	90
slaves, slavery	39, 45, 46, 83, 100, 101, 129
soul	13, 33, 41, 51, 53, 82, 86, 89–91, 94, 96–99, 104, 119, 124–129, 136–139, 141
Sozomen Scholasticus	6
Stoicism	18, 27, 29, 32–34, 43, 44, 54–55, 71
Strobaeus, philosopher	24
suffering	28–29, 40, 42, 44, 52, 54–55, 59, 69–71, 75, 85, 101, 107, 112, 117, 137
Synod of Constantinople (543)	26
Syriac translations	6–8, 61, 79
Theodoret of Cyrus	14
Theonas, bishop of Alexandria	14–15, 17
Thmuis	5–12, 17, 19, 21, 35, 51, 60, 65–66, 75, 89
Thmuitians	5, 6, 11
Thomas, NT figure	100, 101
Tiberius, bishop of Nicaea	6
Titus of Bostra	13–14, 26
torture	24–25, 48, 106–107
Trinity	83
Trinitarian	17
Tropici	7, 10–12
truth	23, 30, 34, 38, 50, 83, 86, 89–90, 92, 100–101, 104–105, 110, 112, 116, 119, 124, 127–128, 132, 136, 141
typology	36–38
Valentinus, heretic	90, 120
Valentinians	118–119
violence	25, 41, 81, 93, 97, 108
violence	27, 40, 81, 93, 97, 108
virtue	24, 28–31, 34, 36, 42–44, 51–53, 55, 59, 70, 75, 86, 91, 94–98, 101, 104, 108, 110, 113, 124, 128, 130, 138
volition	13
war	13, 48–49, 69, 84, 90, 109, 137
Zeno, philosopher	24, 29, 43

Index of Biblical Citations

Old Testament

Gen
- 1:7   36
- 3:1–24   63
- 3:8   83
- 12:1   61, 79
- 14:21   130
- 18:32   79

Exod
- 10:16–17   104
- 12:11   126
- 20:4   122, 127
- 20:13   94, 122, 125
- 20:13–16   122
- 20:17   122
- 32:1   79
- 32:4   127
- 32:7   79
- 32:32   79

Lev
- 19:35–36   125
- 26:12   91

Deut
- 6:4   123, 131
- 6:5   123
- 10:20   82
- 18.15–16a   24, 122
- 30:19   93

Josh
- 1:5   60, 61, 77

3 Kgs
- 20:29   136

4 Kgs
- 1:9–12   133
- 2:23–24   133
- 5:20   101
- 13:21   94

Job
- 31:1   126
- 42:8   79

Ps
- 1:2–3   81
- 2:7   24, 122, 131
- 8:6   132
- 14:1–2 (15:1–2)   128
- 23:7 (24:7)   24, 121
- 26:14 (27:14)   50, 54, 62, 86
- 31:9 (32:9)   125
- 33:15 (34:15)   84
- 36:16 (37:16)   81
- 36:35–36 (37:35–36)   127
- 46:2 (47:1)   135
- 48:1–2 (49:1–2)   135
- 48:17 (49:16)   22, 135
- 48:20 (49:20)   98
- 50:1–2 (51:1–2)   134
- 50:13 (51:13)   132
- 61:10 (62:10)   127
- 62:8 (63:8)   82
- 80:14 (89:13–14)   125
- 104:7 (105:7)   131
- 108:1 (109:1)   133
- 110:1 (111:1)   101
- 110:8 (111:8)   136
- 117:1 (118:1)   24, 121
- 117:3 (118:3)   131
- 126:1 (127:1)   81
- 126:9 (127:9)   125
- 126:11 (127:11)   125
- 126:113 (127:113)   125
- 129:2 (130:2)   112
- 130:1–2 (131:1–2)   83
- 140:3 (141:3)   126
- 145:1 (146:1)   101

Prov
- 4:25   33, 139
- 10:7   86
- 17:1   80
- 28:1   125
- 29:2   86

30:2	129	**New Testament**	
Song		Matt	
1:4	83	1:1	116
5:1	82	2:6	121
5:2	141	2:15	121
Isa		3:2	28, 135
1:3	121	3:3	121
1:19	103	3:8	63
7:14	121	3:13–17	140
9:6	24, 122	3:17	131
14:12	111	4:14	22, 120
26:10	85	5:8	84
35:10	85	5:14	78, 86
40:3	121	5:16	78
40:12	89	5:17	22, 115, 120
51:7	125	5:28	33, 139
66:24	85	6:24	128
Jer		6:33	54, 82
5:21	116	7:15	89
21:8	93	11:28	135
Lam		12:17	22
3:27–28	61, 79	12:45	107
Ezek		13:22	128
16:52	90	16:17	100
33:11	136	16:18	75
Dan		16:19	100
3:24–25	104	16:23	100
Jonah		16:24	103
4:10–11	136	18:8	85
Mic		19	82, 103, 128, 131, 139
5:2	121	19:12	139
Hos		19:17	131
11:1	121	19:21	82, 103
Sir		21	116, 128
9:8	126	21:13	116
21:10	83	22:30	80
		24:5	141
		24:13	51, 86
		25:34	85
		Mark	
		1:1	102, 116
		1:9–11	140
		1:11	131
		1:24	105
		9:43	85

9:48	85	9:1–20	96
10:6	138	Rom	
10:7	138	2:6	119
10:9	138	2:7–9	119
10:18	131	2:16	117
11	116, 128	7:12	124
11:17	116	8:28	119
Luke		10:4	115
1:28	117	12:1	25, 93
1:29	117	13:3	78
1:30–33	117	1 Cor	
3:21–22	140	1:27	98
3:22	131	2:11	24, 120
8:14	128	6:19	91
10:16	116	7:33–34a	82
10:17	101	8:6	131
10:18	111	9:27	39, 101
10:19	62, 84	10:12	112
11:26	107	15:27	132
11:40	139	15:27–28	132
12:19	101	2 Cor	
16:16	117	2:15	124
16:24	115	3:12–4:6	116
16:29	115	5:10	85
16:30	115	5:20	104
16:31	115	6:15	137
18:19	131	6:16	91
19:46	131	Gal	
John		1:13–17	96
1:6–7a	117	Eph	
1:17	136	5:27	92
1:18	121, 131	5:29	137
1:29–34	140	5:31–32	132
1:42	100	6:14	112
4:24	124	Phil	
5:46	116	3:8	46, 77, 141
14:6	89	Col	
14:9	119	1:15	119
17:25	119	1:16	36, 140
20:23	132	3:5	126
Acts		1 Tim	
5:15	94	1:9–10	78
13:10–11	134	1:15	30, 95
5:1–11	134	4:7	113
		6:10	127

2 Tim
  4:7–8   51, 87
  4:10   99
Titus
  2:14   78
Hebrews
  1:1–2   118
  1:3   119, 130–131
  1:6   131
  2:5–8   132
  10:1   136
  10:36   86
  11:31   92
  13:5   60, 77
James
  5:16   84
  5:17–18 56, 78
1 John
  2:22–23 118
Rev
  20:3   83

www.ingramcontent.com/pod-product-compliance
Lightning Source LLC
Chambersburg PA
CBHW041313110526
44591CB00022B/2895